D1722775

SCRIBBLINS

SCRIBBLINS

Stan Drew, Jr.

XULON PRESS

Xulon Press Elite
2301 Lucien Way #415
Maitland, FL 32751
407.339.4217
www.xulonpress.com

Unless otherwise indicated, Scripture quotations taken from the Holy Bible, New International Version (NIV). Copyright © 1973, 1978, 1984, 2011 by Biblica, Inc.™. Used by permission. All rights reserved.

Scripture quotations taken from the King James Version (KJV) – *public domain.*

Scripture quotations taken from the New King James Version (NKJV). Copyright © 1982 by Thomas Nelson, Inc. Used by permission. All rights reserved.

Paperback ISBN-13: 978-1-6628-5781-2
Hardcover ISBN-13: 978-1-6628-5782-9
eBook ISBN-13: 978-1-6628-0906-4

Dedication

THIS BOOK IS dedicated to my wife Lynn, who's love and companionship have been the highlight of my life. Thank you for ending my sentences, begrudgingly laughing at my jokes and supporting me in this and all my endeavors. Surely, your reward is in heaven.

Introduction

AVAST YE SCALAWAGS! 'Tis me seventieth revolution around the sun. So as a means of introduction, a story befitting this grand achievement is necessary and, as usual, uncalled for . . . and, of course, it comes with a small fee, which has become me custom. So, gather round, mateys, and raise a glass (or perhaps a cup of pulverized beans) to the morning and pay me the attention I surely don't deserve on this, the seventieth year of my existence!

I wasn't supposed to be here, they say, though, clearly, those who wished me dead weren't in charge of me demise or just weren't very good shots. Certainly, me own attempts to hail the hearse were broadly misunderstood. Though I partook of the white "powdered" keg, me main drug of choice was me own adrenaline. Most don't really understand life on the "high seas" unless encumbered by their own poor choices. I was, indeed, a pirate, stealing time and collecting treasure beyond the normal excesses. I have less and less recollection of those times, which, thankfully, keeps me sane.

At this stage of the game, it appears I have sailed past the wreckage that was me self-imposed destiny. I was initially drawn to the rocks by the siren's call and the plentiful barrels of drink, but for reasons only known to the God of heaven, I was plucked from that particular ship of fools, unlike so many others. For some unfathomable reason, I find meself still afloat and ready for whatever adventures lie ahead, be they medically necessary or determined by the wind.

It should be noted that I love the sea. I retired to it, having never really explored it beyond a few cruises to places that actually are viewed better from the sea. There were, of course, a number of deep-sea adventures that caught me chasing seafood and sunsets just off the coast with a rod and reel. Still, I am drawn to it like clouds to the horizon. I am, in terms of what a child aspires to be in his golden years, a pirate with little or no regard for whatever mistakes I was allowed, as thus far, none have been fatal. I am enjoying the treasures hidden in these years, most assuredly as golden as they were predicted to be by those who attach precious metals and stones to occasions.

Me wife and me first mate (one and the same) built our seaside retirement home on a large tidal body of water known as Crescent Lake, in northeast Florida, once a place where pirates came to repair their ships . . . or so the story goes.

At the south end of the lake is a small but navigable creek known as "Haw Creek" that empties into a much smaller lake. That lake is aptly named "Dead Lake," so named as a port for pirate ships "deadheading" for routine maintenance or recovering from battles at sea. There is ample room there to anchor and accept delivery of supplies via dry land, if needed. Certainly, pirate ships would have been able to "dead end" there for repairs and resupply, so the story is believable. That is true and readable history according to local legend and the restaurant menu from which I extracted it, which, in these parts, is the absolute gospel.

As for my pirate-like appearance, there are some similarities. Of course, I do not wear a tri-cornered hat as those went out with the British from which they were stolen, and the eye patch was removed when the powder burns healed in the great 1976

Bicentennial conflict at which I was the official firework holder and lighter.

At first glance, you'd likely notice the limp. It's not a peg leg exactly. It is a completely replaced hip joint, which, if you know about replaced hips, you also know that they drive a peg (of sorts) down into the femur and insert what is best explained as a trailer hitch into what used to be your hip joint—hence, me pegged leg. I don't always limp, but it does tend to happen a little more in cold or rainy weather. I try not to "Aaarrrr" too much in winter, but Aaarrrrthritis is me mortal enemy. The peg leg is sufficient for me needs, me sea legs being as stable as any at me now officially "advanced" age.

Me spine is somewhat bent from the lifting and loading of cannon balls and climbing to the crow's nest on rougher seas, which is not exactly true but infers that it was a tool and routinely abused for my work. I worked hard. The miracle-working sawbones have made valiant attempts to straighten it, and I consider their efforts great successes. I can't complain as long as I am still tall enough to ride the rides and dance with the fair (and still comely) lady who co-owns the vessel and seaside cottage. A crooked spine is better than a crooked spyglass. One will keep you humble; the other will keep you lost.

As you would expect from an old, scaley pirate, thar be a parrot on me shoulder, but you won't see it. It squawks at me constantly and has for years . . . kinda guiding me away from my tendencies to perform the mischief for which I was once famous. Me thinks I have a bit of the Sparrow in me, though I have never been known to run with the Heard. (Shuddup! That's hilarious!)

An accident while in the service of me now much-maligned country took the majority of me pearly whites, but the replacements are plastic, which is a far better choice given the splinters that come with wooden ones. This also assures that me mates won't be trying to steal them in the event of me untimely death, which could occur at any moment, depending on certain drug interactions or God's perfect justice.

I have a scruffy beard most of the time . . . mainly because, like most pirates, I have no interest in grooming beyond the requisite showers (required by me first mate, sometimes cook and Chief Odor Detector.) The pocket t-shirts and cargo shorts that have become my fanciful, albeit desperate "look," are both interchangeable and can also be worn with suspenders or sash, depending on me audience. I wear pickleball shoes because to call them tennis shoes at my age and function is altogether inappropriate. (Oh, the hilarity!)

I had a bout with rum in me early years but have found that sobriety fits me better as I've aged. Stumbling aboard ship requires at least some knowledge of the length and width of the deck and the location of the masts. The odds are that I probably wouldn't still be here had that particular demon not been robbed of me all too willing soul.

At this point, I'm aware of the need to reconcile with whatever and whomever identifies as polite society. I can, without too much trouble, allow meself to be somewhat genteel and very nearly eloquent when in the company of those who identify as sensitive, though there are no guarantees of language should a fight erupt or a breaking wave demands attention.

Me ship is a mast-less eighteen-foot bay boat that allows me first mate and I to scurry about the lake searching for whales and tall tales . . . always docking at the port of 3 Bananas for a bite of local sea urchin or whatever it is beneath that battered and deep-fried crust.

Me first mate is often called on to assist in righting the ship. Thar be no more loyal mate on this nor any other ship. She could have her own ship or choice of captains if she wanted, but she prefers Cap'n Scragglebeard for some odd reason known only to her and a mighty and ever-laughing God.

So here I be, another year's sailing toward the eternity that calls us all. I am none the worse for wear, depending, of course, on the weather and the most recent lab results. I have no particular target date for my voyage to the great beyond because I have learned that there are only two options: wake up, set a course, raise the mainsail and follow the wind, or accept the plank and the keel-haul that follows the mutiny of the crew. Thar ain't a lot of choices beyond those.

I stand ready for either alternative, facing into the wind, cutlass at my side, the ship's wheel in hand, braving the waves that still shift the sands of time, and daring any of them to drag me down to the briny depths where the devil reigns supreme.

It is neither courage nor adventure that drives me forward. It is the grace and mercy of the everlasting God. I stand bent slightly forward before the God of creation, knowing full well that my journey ends in His presence despite my efforts to avoid His tender mercies! I have surely collected the bounty I did not deserve, if only counted in years above this ever-churning sea of life.

So, let the celebration begin, but certainly my time aboard this spinning dirt and sea cannot be credited to my own doing. I had no hand in my longevity nor am I worthy of these now mostly peaceful and calming seas. I am merely a servant of the King, ever dependent on Him for the breath that has thus far withstood the momentum of time and the winds of change. Onward toward the horizon! Yo-ho-ho and a bottle of Tums!

Psalm 146:6

He is the Maker of heaven and earth, the sea, and everything in them—he remains faithful forever.

The Map

THE BEST WAY to navigate a collection of writings of this sort is to identify each one and classify them according to topic and general mood. In that vein, I've devised this map that will assist you in that effort There is no particular order to the entries as they are written over time, sometimes years between them. Mainly, though, I want this to be an enjoyable book, so feel free to laugh a lot, cry a little, and enjoy the journey. Fair winds!

Generally speaking, like any compass, these are efforts to provide direction. The needle always points skyward as that is the direction we'd most like to point when considering our future home. Yes, I write about heaven.

What could indicate funny more than a laughing skull? Unless, of course, you already knew that the crossed bones are each a humurus (Hopefully, that won't be the best example of that sort of comedy relief.)

The candle is doing what it is intended to do . . . shedding a little light on lessons learned from personal experiences as well as evoking reflections and fond memories of people and events.

Hopefully, the spyglass will cause the reader to look a bit deeper into the subject matter. It brings distant images closer than we might otherwise imagine and provides a clearer objective.

The quill pen designates a fictional tale intended to inspire and encourage, generally with a moral and often written with an imaginative flair and a purposed, albeit invented encounter.

The magnifying glass highlights Scripture from the previous entry . . . It's highlighted for a reason. Think on these. These will never return empty.

Damascus

I MET AN ANGEL once in a now forgotten club, somewhere in Dallas, Texas. Yeah, I know what you're thinking when you hear that, but read the story anyway. It may help to know that there are powers much higher than our own.

I refer to him as "Damascus" because it's a cool angel name, and there's an actual road trip story attached to it. I never really knew his name. This isn't the story of my conversion, but it is the story of the road I was on and the circumstances that made me begin the journey back to a place of contentment.

I can't really make any assertions that would convince anyone of the angel claim, but I can speak to the truth of it. I really don't want to tell this story, but truth-telling is a tough business. Life ain't all excellent adventures, and sometimes you just lose control of the joystick.

Compared to my experiences with personal demons, I assure you that an angel was a rare sighting—if indeed he was an angel. I had entertained the former and was headed for a permanent engagement. It's been over fifty years since this particular event, so I've had time to review it all, time and again. I'm convinced of my conclusion. Whether you agree is up to you, but the evidence points to a meeting with an actual messenger from a place none of us has been and few of us are going.

You probably think of angels as mythical beings fluttering around, watching your every move, or some little mini-you that sits on your shoulder and whispers directions while you muddle through life and pay more attention to the little devil on the other shoulder. That's the theatrical version. You may even sing about them at Christmas, but I actually believe they exist, not as deities but rather as messengers. They shouldn't be worshiped. They answer to God. They are created beings. They can and do interact with folks. Angels and demons exist. I believe because I've had occasion to encounter both, this tale being one of those occasions.

There's biblical evidence for angels, and I believe they can literally be dispatched. I believe one was sent to me at a time when I was pretty well lost in the world. I also believe that many people prayed for me most of my life, mostly because I was a hard case.

I had no real sense of fear or caution. I don't know if it was a complete lack of maturity or a somewhat suppressed death wish, but I do know I enjoyed life beyond what I should have, but I didn't respect it. I lived beyond my means and above my station. I was that free spirit you've heard so much about. The problem was, there was more than one, and those spirits were at war.

I believe in God. It seems like I always have, but there was a time that I literally dared Him. I didn't realize that was what I was doing, but as I look back on it, I pushed the limits of what I knew to be right. I knew that was a battle I couldn't win. Yet, I continued to pursue things that flew in the face of all that I believed.

Could it be that He did send an actual angel—a warning—an event that would cause me to take another look at life in general and how I fit into the grand scheme? I believe that He could and perhaps did. I cannot demand that God sent an angel to assist me, but I must accept the possibility.

Nothing else actually puts me in the place I eventually landed. Nothing else could possibly have begun the sequence of events that would steer me to a place of self-examination in the middle of a giant wave meant to crush me, leaving me without so much as a flotation device.

You see, I navigated the world on my own by myself, mostly, or so I thought. I had no real compass, nor did I think I needed one. I left the battlefield that was my home at an early age. My parents were both great people and good parents despite their dislike for one another. Due to some (unknown to me) flagrant violation of their vows by one or the other, they mutually agreed to divorce when I was sixteen. I can't say I was surprised. Until then, they did the best they could, staying together for the sake of the children and all of that.

At this point, it would be an understatement to say that I was a bit overdrawn at the bank of mellow due to what teachers and others called my excess of "nervous energy." I just had no way to burn it all off. I was cursed with a somewhat faulty fuel gauge. The mix wasn't always precise. The testosterone to adrenaline ratio would sometimes require an indeterminate amount of pharmaceutical additive to keep me running without bursting into flames. These were becoming more available in those days, but I refrained for some reason until such time as I became an adult.

My mom remarried fairly soon after the divorce, and my dad moved to another side of town. Another authority figure just wasn't something that appealed to me, so I was caught somewhere between what really was and what might've been. Consequently, I struck out on my own, content with whatever curse or blessing might follow. It was the seventies. Things were changing.

There were no promises beyond my next job and no future if I didn't personally build one. I actually finished high school while living on my own, conveniently escaping the realities of the world without the benefit of dependence on anything more than my unfocused self. These were all hidden assets, or at least I considered them that. I neither respected authority nor contended with it.

It's a long, not overly sad story from there, one that doesn't necessarily need to be detailed any further than to describe my intent to take the world on without the benefit of a properly designed guidance system. Suffice to say, I was hard pressed to do the right thing because I didn't know the right thing, even though I had been "trained up in the way that I should go" for more Sundays than most seminary students. I had complete disregard for any direction given me.

I kind've understood the pyramid scheme of life: school, military, wife, kids, job, family, house, divorce, drugs, alcohol, early death—you know, the American dream. I made every effort to live up to my own expectations filled with the knowledge that I was pretty much a failed experiment. What I failed at mostly was getting those life experiences in the proper order. I just couldn't get it right.

I never allowed myself to be unhappy, though. I'm not sure if that was a built-in defense system or just something that kept me motivated to try to be what I couldn't, which was happy. Yes, I know, It was quite the conundrum. I really didn't know or understand the difference. With happiness came intermittent sorrow. Who knew? I needed perpetual happiness. I expected a much smoother path to tranquility. I opted to join the club and earn my frequent flier miles in the clubs, taverns, honkey-tonks, dive bars, or pubs of wherever I was headed.

One day, through some twisting of fate and varying degrees of indecision, I found myself in Dallas, Texas, working another futureless job and looking for the next party, which was my real job. Unlike my hometown of Atlanta, I didn't know the good side of town from the bad, so I made friends in both.

Someone gave me tickets to see Dwight Yoakam at a local club. The details of my interest in that event fail me, but on that particular evening, I started early, which was my custom when preparing for events. I'd probably get a bite to eat after work and drive to some seedy location, looking for the young entrepreneur who would provide me with the fuel I needed to restore my "normal" level of confidence. I rarely had to look for good times. They always found me!

I scored some magic dust somewhere around Harry Hines Blvd. The fact that I hadn't been beaten to death or shot during the acquisition process was a good sign. I was feeling better than usual, so I started to imbibe at just the right hour. This was normally a fairly mechanical process, tried and tested over years of pursuing the dream. I was comfortable with my plan.

The (Jägermeister) shooters at the first establishment were particularly effective, but I was pretty good at gauging my own level of euphoria. I was generally able to light the fuse at just the right time, only this time, it appeared as though I would be taking the bullet train. I found myself rising higher to the occasion than usual. Perhaps another taste of the magic dust would help me past the initial launch. Staggering to the restroom, I once again partook of the now volatile cure for whatever ailed me. That second dose sometimes mellowed me and made the ride smoother. Not so, in this case.

The magic dust was a little purer than I was used to, and I started to peak a little early. That could be a bad situation, so I braced for the hyperdrive ride to whatever universe I'd be visiting. I was still in command of the experience, but that situation quickly evaporated. Thinking this shouldn't be happening so quickly, I was relatively assured that this was going to be a sloppy night, for sure. That was somewhat of a disappointment, but here I was. No turning back now. Maybe another drink would help. My bad choices were multiplying at the speed of incoherence. If you've never been there, just hold your horses.

I made it to the club somehow because I was traveling at much higher speeds than the world around me. I limped into the bar rather than my usual confident, striding entrance, as I had no real bearings. I was a bit confused, to say the least, and made a completely swaggerless entrance. I stumbled in without anyone noticing and found a seat at the bar. I was immediately at home there. I was practiced at masking my inebriated state and apparently had snuck in without garnering too much attention. I was able to order without too much effort, but I was literally holding on for dear life. Even I didn't believe I was unable to navigate the simple act of . . . anything.

The night was young, but I was about ten sheets into a blizzard by the time ol' Dwight came on stage. I remember barely seeing him and applauding but not much else. I'm not sure that my hands even touched together. I struck up several conversations with folks who really had no idea why I was talking to them or what I was saying. I had morphed into that guy, the one no one wants to be.

That's when the angel appeared. I knew because he couldn't have been anything else, as my level of communication was far too disrupted to actually converse with another earthling. He just kinda sidled up to me in a Texas friendly way and tried to have a normal conversation. He took the seat next to me which was cleared for obvious reasons. Stupid is contagious in a bar, and no one really wanted to associate with the one wearing the smile or trying to stir his drink with his finger and catch the stirrer with his tongue.

I remember not being able to talk and just staring at him or maybe his hat. He was full-on Texan, drawl and all. I spit out a few garbled sentences, and it went down something like this:

"Hey pardner . . . Whassh goin' on wishu?"

The first thing he said was, "I've been right where you're sittin'."

Suddenly, I was aware of how bad it had gotten and that I was losing control.

"I doubt that, and I ain't complainin'."

Then, oddly enough, I put together the most perfect sentences I'd ever spoken. "I just need to stop. I've been doing this too long," I said, clear as a bell, the first complete sentence in hours. It was an absolute revelation to me. I couldn't imagine how those words had come out of my mouth. Self- examination wasn't on my list of character traits.

"Yep. You sure have," he said as if he knew me already. "There's a way out, though," he said without missing a beat.

He was casual about it, not at all judgmental. I'm telling you there was an aura about him, something only I could see. I didn't really pay attention to it, but looking back, I realize that he moved through the crowd without effort. He came directly for me with one intention. I'm certain of this. He was there to guide me to a place of deliverance. I cannot remember his face or anything about him except his hat.

"Can I buy you a beer or something?" I asked, making sure I didn't sound too familiar or less manly than the rodeo clown I had suddenly become. I always bought the drinks, especially if I was almost broke.

"Nope. I've had my share, but I'd imagine you're not through yet."

"You're right about that!" I ordered up another and a shooter to boot.

"You drivin'?" he asked kind of casually.

"I reckon so," I said. "I don't know who else to call, and I'm almost outta' money, but I've got enough gas to get to work tomorrow." I laughed again at my honest admission.

"Why don't you give me your keys and let me take you somewhere so you can come down a little. From the looks of it, you've been hittin' it perty hard. You may need to tap the brakes a little."

I smiled and nodded, fumbled in my pocket, held out my keys, then kicked back the last shot I'd have for a long while.

Then came the fade to black. I do not remember a single moment beyond that. I had always held my liquor beyond what would be considered normal capacity. I guess that's why they call them "shots." I don't even remember the lights being turned on or the attempts to resuscitate me . . . none of that. Apparently, the blast had sent me directly into a black hole. I had done the incomprehensible. I had overdosed, and it wasn't pretty.

I woke up sometime the next day worried about losing my job. I was nearly blind, not just from the hangover, but there was something wrong. I really couldn't see out of either eye. I tried to cover one to see if that improved anything, but nope. I was blind. Everything was more than just fuzzy. I wasn't sure if I had been in an accident or not. I literally couldn't see anything but the hazy lights, and I could hear voices.

I begged God not to leave me blind. I told him I would change this time. "Just don't leave me blind, Lord. I can't be bli—I just can't. Dear God. NO. PLEASE NO!"

"You hungry?" spoke the sweetest Texas drawl I'd ever heard.

"Yes ma'am." I thought maybe I was in heaven. Maybe I died somewhere last night. Food sounded like a good idea.

"Let me get you a menu, sugar."

"I can't see" I sort of slurred in response.

A brief moment passed, and I heard a zipper opening to my right. It sounded like thunder in my ear. A menu appeared right in front of my face with a hand attached to it. I could see the hand . . . and the menu. How odd was that? I was blind just a second ago.

At that moment, I realized I was in an oxygen tent surrounded by medical personnel and hooked up to many machines, wondering where Dwight and that dude who somehow knew my condition might be. This was all new to me.

But at least I wasn't blind, so the answer to a prayer had already occurred, but I will admit that I started counting body parts before I said the necessary prayer of thanksgiving, the rote, praise given a not really existent God in the midst of some miraculous discovery; in this case, survival.

"Thank you, Jesus!"

Someone in the room laughed. I guess my euphoria at discovering I wasn't sightless was a bit loud.

The drawl girl spoke again. "Do you want some coffee?"

"More than anything." I still had a bit of a slur.

"Hold on a sec. I'll need to unplug you."

So, I guessed I was getting up. I wasn't sure that was a good idea. I didn't know if I still had all my internal organs or if there were stitches or anything.

She came over and removed the tent. Apparently, I'd had breathing issues. She hooked a bag to an IV transport stand and helped me get up. Then, she walked me to the hallway coffee station.

I felt fine but needed the coffee. She helped me pour it because I was pretty weak but not so weak that I couldn't dump the sugar and cream into the cup. I noticed she only poured a half of a cup. I waited. She looked at me and said sweetly, "If I fill that cup up, you're going to spill half of it. You're shaking pretty bad."

I hadn't really noticed. I shook a lot of mornings. I'd been running somewhere close to terminal velocity for a while. I did notice that this woman knew more about me than I really ever allowed. She was very sweet, though, and older than me, probably in her fifties. I was in my late thirties.

She introduced herself as Sue Brown. I responded with "I'm whatever is written on that chart in there, or at least I will be after this coffee."

She chuckled and said, "What do you remember about last night?"

I did a bit of a double take and said, "It's too soon to know. I actually need the coffee. It helps me remember. How much do you know?" I laughed, but I was dead serious, which was a lot better than just dead.

"Well," she started slowly. "You overdosed on what appeared to be a high-grade cocaine product and quite a bit of alcohol. You also had some pain medication that helped you along, best we can tell. You're lucky to have all your functions this morning."

She continued, "The young man who came in with you had already performed CPR on you at the bar you were in. The paramedics kept you breathing until you got here, and we started bringing you down early this morning. You had some violent physical reactions.

We pumped your stomach and slowed you down gradually. It wasn't pretty. Have you ever overdosed before?

"No. It's not something I do regularly. I try not to projectile vomit or convulse in public. It tends to scare children and takes me out of the dating circuit."

She laughed because she had to, as did others in the room. I was slowly getting back on the horse.

She handed me a pill in a cup, Librium I think. I assumed it was to keep me calm during the recovery process. I was a walking PDR, so I sort of knew the process. It wasn't long before I began to rest, but before I did, I asked about the young man she had spoken of earlier.

"He didn't give his name, and he left as soon as he heard you would be okay. He drove here in your car. He was wearing a hat, a really nice Stetson. That's all anyone here remembered, but he saved your life."

I thought about that a lot. I knew he'd been a patient there, but no one remembered him. I know nothing about him and probably never will. This story is the only thanks I can offer other than to give the glory to God for sending someone to my aid.

I went on to rehab there in the hospital for the next thirty days. I'm not sure that I accepted the entire program. I continued to drink after that, but I never drank the same, and I never touched cocaine again, which was quite a feat considering my propensity to indulge in it.

I moved from Texas to California and tried to straighten up without any assistance beyond AA and NA programs. It was tough, but I was able to walk through it all. It felt like I had help, even though I didn't quite understand it.

Somewhere in the back of my mind, I am always aware that someone watches over me. There's a peace about it. I see folks all the time who remind me of that angel who saved my life. Maybe he wasn't an angel at all. Maybe he was just a kind soul who intervened on my behalf. All I know is what I've written here.

Now and again, I wear my own cool hat. It's the one I wear in my author's photo. It's not as nice as the Damascus's Stetson because, for sure, I don't fit the angel profile. But this much I do know, there's a lot of folks out there who don't know how deep they've dug the hole. I just try to point the way back because I've been right where they're sittin'.

I keep this verse with me to remind me that there's folks out there I've never met, and they're all at different stages of barely hangin' on. My job is to be kind to all of 'em and do my best to point 'em to Jesus. I ain't no angel, but I do know the way home. It's a rocky road for some of us.

Hebrews 13:2

Do not forget to show hospitality to strangers, for by so doing some people have shown hospitality to angels without knowing it.

First Kiss of Death

WHEN I WAS about twelve years old, I met my older sister's best friend's little sister. Her name was Patty, and she was gorgeous. She was my age, blond hair, blue eyes, and would sneak off with me to the side yard and talk about everything that mattered, which, at that age, was anything that kept her talking.

We both liked bugs. She more than I, as I will soon explain. The basement entrance was on the side of the house, so we could venture inside and study the various insects that scurried about when the door was opened. It was altogether a working relationship. We were able to study the habits of quite a few bugs and would talk about their varying degrees of size, color, and ways they would kill their prey, young entomologist that we were.

One day while poking around in the red clay with a stick trying to find roly-polies, also known as pill bugs, she asked me if I wanted to kiss her. I responded a lot slower than I normally did because my tongue swelled up in my mouth for some reason. I must have had a stroke of some sort because I was suddenly staring at my brain, I guess because my eyes rolled back into my head.

After a brief moment of whatever medical emergency I'd just experienced, I responded "yes" in a very weak and high-pitched voice, one that all but proved my less than manly frailties. I immediately regretted having answered out loud, but at least I had done so without spewing the pint or so of saliva that had suddenly built up in my mouth.

Apparently, the relationship had changed in a way that took me by surprise. I had no idea about how to treat these Femalian creatures. No one had ever taught me. The only examples I had outside of school were my sister and mom and girls at church, so this was uncharted territory. I wasn't sure what to do, so I waited for a sign.

She leaned forward and pressed her mouth against mine, just enough so that I could feel her teeth. I opened my mouth and turned my head just like Errol Flynn and all those other manly men who stole the hearts of the ever-fainting damsels saved from distress or dat stress or whatever. It was a short kiss, but there was a moment of flicking tongues that caused me to forever remember this particular moment, a small, hard, bb-like charm was apparently swapped in the process. I swallowed it quickly, not knowing if this was some strange adult thing, or if it was just a piece of her gum.

I kneeled there for a moment and tried to gather my wits. My tongue, now a giant, overly inflated knot, was detached in some strange way, and my throat had closed due to the foreign piece of baloney that had just invaded my mouth. I didn't know tongues were involved. I tried not to act as if I was mortally wounded or anything like that, so I mustered up a look that must have been somewhere between choking to death and eternal bliss. I don't know what that looks like either, but it was my first attempt at being "suave and debonair," words I had only heard at the Madison Theater when Clark Gable or Humphrey Bogart would respond to any of the Femalian species.

Just as I was about to speak, it happened. Patty, now the girl of my dreams, found a roly-poly and picked it up with her fingers, which made it roll itself into a ball. Then, she just popped it into her mouth as if it were a Raisinette or a Malted Milk Ball. I just stared in amazement at what I had just seen. The girl with whom I had shared my first kiss had just devoured one of my friends. I was appalled but also curious. Then, without flinching, she found another one and popped it into her mouth. I remembered the bb-like object she had deposited in my mouth. I was pretty sure it wasn't dead or digestible.

Watching her eat that little bug was one thing. Hearing the crunch was quite another. I tried not to show my disgust, but then she found another one and offered it to me like we were sharing popcorn. I politely declined and left the basement without so much as a word, trying not to heave or show any signs of wanting to projectile vomit this now implanted, alien creature from whatever organ it had taken hostage in order to lay its eggs or which artery it would attach itself to and begin the process of sucking my blood until my forehead dented in. Needless to say, I was flipping out a bit.

After the shock wore off and the entire universe, as I knew it, drifted back into proper alignment, and gravity began to act responsibly enough to keep me grounded, I walked with her back to the picnic table and took a seat on one of the benches. I was stuck somewhere between cloud nine and the seventh circle of hell. I had no option but to ask her about the kiss and the subsequent devouring of one of our mutual friends. First things first. Did she enjoy the kiss? She said it was okay and that I was a good kisser. I internally thanked every movie star who'd ever instructed me. Then, I asked about the bug. Had she, in fact, put one in my mouth?

"Yes," she said. "I wanted to share them with you. I eat them whenever I find them. They're crunchy and good!" That's when I noticed a little bit of whitish, maybe yellowish bug guts still on the bottom lip I had just enjoyed. My stomach churned. I was certain that I had just had an experience with an alien being. What else could have taken me so quickly through that range of emotions?

When her dad came to pick her up that day, I was a bit sad but relieved that I would never again have to watch that disturbing scene again except in the nightmares that would surely follow. Patty and I were doomed from the very start. My first kiss was a disaster, a memory never to be forgotten. It was a considerable length of time before I was able to kiss again, probably a couple of months, but that didn't matter. I was twelve with no girlfriend.

I tried to get over the entire event, but it was pretty much devastating to my normal, almost teenage sensibilities. The juxtaposition of those two images was enough to up my movie game from watching swashbuckling romance tales to horror/monster movies. At least I could predict the ending.

I avoided Patty like a wasp's nest after that. I just couldn't put the beauty and the sound of crunching insects in the same place in my head. I hid the experience in the back of my mind somewhere near liver and onions and a badly stubbed skateboard toe. My mother became concerned that I wasn't looking for love and even questioned why I wouldn't respond to Patty's advances. I just couldn't tell the story, not ever, not until now.

I heard from Patty a few years later. It was like pouring gasoline on an old flame. Her voice was raspy and hard. I imagined that was a consequence of her diet. It was a short conversation. I actually feared another alien encounter, so I made a quick excuse in an effort to avoid too much conversation.

Some years later, I was at the drive-in theater with my wife. Something about the sound of the popcorn caused me to flash back to that time in the basement with Patty. I was about to tell her the story when she turned toward me. At that moment, the light from the movie screen flashed across her face. There was a bit of a glint allowing me to spot a little piece of popcorn kernel hull on her lip. The flashback was immediate. I lost it completely. I impulsively threw my Coke in her face and ran from the car screaming. I missed the ending of *Creature from the Black Lagoon*.

I never tried to explain it, not even to the in-laws or the lawyers who described the scene as a "Coke-fueled assault with malice aforethought" in the ultimate legal proceedings. That little episode cost me a split-level house and a good dog.

To this day, when my more stable wife eats popcorn, I'm able to find my way outside to avoid any conflict that might arise. We maintain a vigorous pest control program that prevents anything that flies, rolls itself into a ball, slithers, crawls, or might be edible from entering our home. Thus far, that strategy has worked and most of the nightmares have long since subsided.

Still, though, I worry that I might have PTSD (Pill bugs Threatening Stan's Digestion) or some other weird psychological disorder as a result of my first encounter with this kissing cannibal. I fear x-rays that might expose a giant roly-poly attached to my spine or some other body-snatching encounter.

I stepped on a Palmetto bug on the porch this morning. I heard the all too familiar crunch. I never looked back. I just kept walking through the valley of the shadow of death. Patty's face flashed into my head. It's been over half a century, but it still haunts me. Some things just stick with you, I guess.

My mother told me later that Patty had moved to Bangkok, Thailand, with her husband and had become a chef of some renown. I tried not to gag thinking what she might present as food in that environment. Perhaps roly-polies are a delicacy there, or perhaps that is where the alien hive is gathering.

Protect your children.

Master of Disguise

I'M CONCERNED THAT I may not present myself accurately. I may not have painted the word picture of who I am in real life. I've been thinking about that a lot, and I wanted to take a moment to expose what may have been misleading. I want to create something that portrays me as the person I really am and not just some persona wearing a disguise to fool people into thinking I'm something I'm not.

I am somewhat disguised most of the time. Although I have no particular advantage in the area of disguise, I wear one anyway. It keeps me out of trouble. I'm not one to hide those things that might invoke fear and trembling or cause small children to get off my lawn without my having to show my "curmudgenous" inclinations, so I thought it necessary to point out a few specific issues that bring together my clever and oft-used disguise.

The first thing you see are the glasses. I wear glasses because I can't see to hit the cup with my coffee or thread the fishing line through my hook. That condition extends into other areas where vision is an extremely important tool. Rather than go into great detail, the lid is raised in the facility for a reason. Don't complain that it is up, and make sure I'm wearing my glasses if you see me headed in that direction, particularly if you're next in line. Live streaming once had a completely different meaning.

I wear a hat because I'm losing my hair. That makes no sense to me any more than a comb-over solves any problem associated with that loss. I cannot find any reason for the depletion of hair. I'm sure there's an associated degree program that allows one to study such phenomenon, but I'm not nearly that inquisitive of the follicular sciences. I also wear the hat so that I won't experience oozing scalp blisters from the unrelenting Florida sun. For the curious, fish can see forehead glare, so there's that as well.

I have three hats, each with its own embroidered inscription: Ford, Camouflage, and University of Georgia. I actually purchased the UGA hat in Georgia. I was a fan back before the "Great Awokening," when tenses made sense and red hats weren't a political statement.

The black Ford hat is an impulse purchase because I'd left my hat at home and needed something to cover my head. I happened to see it while getting an oil change at the Ford dealership, back before they made the decision to move their plant to Mexico from Ohio, almost requiring me to retire it, but it's a hat, not an idol I use for worship.

The camouflage hat is so people won't see me when I pull off the road and run into the woods for obvious reasons. There are not enough restrooms between my house and the closest town. Using the jug is far too dangerous and requires far more dexterity than I can muster while driving, so I prefer the sprint to the woods (if you can imagine an older man with a trailer hitch for a hip actually sprinting across culverts).

Then, there's my "Groucho" brows, aptly named so that I can align my disguise with the appropriate Marx (there also being Marxists with whom I do not agree). I'm still not sure about these eyebrows or their sudden tendency to not only grow like weeds, but it appears some of them have also decided to relocate to places they shouldn't go. Sometimes one will get away, and I will find it up on my forehead or on the bridge of my nose acting as if it has gained some sort of independence from the rest. I'm not sure why this concerns me. Apparently, I require order in the brow ranks. I'm sure there's a psychological disorder named for that, probably with an obsessive-compulsive component that will be used to place me into the home along with a list of other mental failures. I rue the day.

Speaking of rogue hair, some of it has decided, on its own, to grow into my ears, yet another mystery that evades any sort of scientific conclusion. I can only imagine that the hair is there so that I can't actually hear death sneaking up on me. It makes no sense otherwise. It has a will of its own, like the eyebrow hairs. I worry that they are all in league, conspiring to create a path for warts or other dermatological nightmares.

My beard is somewhat of a chore that has become a daily, forced exercise in grooming, something I don't want to spend a lot of time on in my retirement except maybe to keep the biscuit dust and dried soup from becoming an embarrassment to my wife. So I use the trimmer on occasion while allowing the beast to still hide the half-century of shaving accidents and ever-present, reddish-brown hint of barbecue sauce and gravy badges of honor. "Scruffy" best describes this part of the disguise.

All of these components come together to present to the world the appearance of a good ol' Southern boy with a wealth of living under his belt and a penchant for cracking jokes, laughing at the world as it implodes around him, an aging patriot of the first order, dedicated to the causes that made him what he is today: an old, penitent sinner, enjoying the fading wealth of a once great nation now moving in the direction of those ideas that will surely dissolve her once high standing in the world.

But in actuality, I'm just a good ol' Southern boy with a wealth of living under his belt and a penchant for cracking jokes, laughing at the world as it implodes around me...an aging patriot of the first order, dedicated to the causes that made me what I am today...an old, penitent sinner, enjoying the waning wealth of a once great nation, now moving in the direction of those ideas that will surely dissolve her once high standing in the world.

Maybe I'm not disguised at all. Maybe what you see is what you get.

2 Corinthians 5 :14

Therefore, if any man be in Christ, he is a new creature: old things are passed away; behold, all things are become new.

Spellcheck

"LORD, YOU KNOW I have these spells, these times when I push away from you, these times when I think I can just go it alone without inviting you to the contest or acknowledging your presence, times when I just head out into the open water on my own and attempt to conquer whatever comes. I know you must laugh when I stare into the abyss and yell, 'I've got this!' because I never do. Thank you for your faithfulness, even when I am not."

On reflection, it's like when I first learned to swim on Jackson Lake. I remember holding onto my dad's arm and treading water just like he'd taught me. He'd shown me how to do everything, and I was determined to swim on my own. He was fully aware of my stubbornness. He was my dad. He knew a lot more about me than I did.

We jumped off the dock together, and I did just as he had instructed. I trusted him, but I still held onto his arm as I received my final instructions. The moment of truth was near, and fear was not an option.

In my mind, I felt like I could swim across the entire lake. It was only a mile or so. All I had to do was follow the instructions. I pushed off from the dock piling and released my grip on the only thing between me and certain death. I was on my own, finally free to—I sank like a mud-filled boot.

I had a moment to think it all through. I'd done all the right things. I'd kicked really hard and cupped my hands in order to scoop away the water. I had moved my arms in a near-perfect circular motion.

No way could I be doing anything wrong. I had this, but down I went like a pirate cannon in the wake of a fierce battle. There I was, sinking to the depths. How could this be?

The water was murky but clear enough that I could open my eyes. It was a bit scary down there. I didn't know how far I'd gone or if my dad was still close enough to save me from my failed attempt. I thought about all the huge catfish we'd pulled out of the lake and what else might be down there to eat me, but I was pretty sure my dad was still close. He wouldn't leave me out there to die. He was my father.

I could see myself struggling, arms flailing around like some drunk guy waving down a taxi and legs kicking and churning up the bubbles and mud from the bottom. That's when I recognized that I was pretty helpless, just another stone headed for the rocky bottom.

I was still trying to figure out what went wrong when I saw that big, anchor-tattooed forearm coming at me from above. I was retrieved almost instantly, though it seemed like an eternity. I was mostly unaffected except for the damage to my pride. I was still determined to figure it all out and return to the depths if necessary. Obstinance and tenacity overtook any semblance of prudence. Clearly, this trait was not yet developed enough to distinguish between determination and foolishness. That issue remained into adulthood.

I went out again and again, each time a little further, each time a little less afraid. Still, he was there to get me back on track when I would go under. He was patient with me. The more times I went out, the farther I swam. With practice, my fear turned to confidence. My dad's instruction and patience with me became a source of gratitude.

I learned to swim that day. I also learned that I had limitations. I learned a little about faith and faithfulness. I accepted that I couldn't have learned how to swim without the help of my father. That was true about a lot of things. Young men need fathers.

It's been over sixty years since that day I went out on my own into the deep, that day I understood all that could go wrong but did it my way, anyway, that day I thought I could go the distance without him, that day I took it upon myself to conquer water, that day I recognized how deep I could go without help.

My earthly dad is no longer here to save me from my foolishness or teach me the ways of the world, but he did instruct me about my Father in heaven. He did point me in the direction I needed to go. I am secure in my relationship with Him. I am grateful for those times when He reaches down and pulls me out of the abyss. I've learned to trust Him. I've learned of His faithfulness and His love for me. I have learned to talk with Him and take His instruction. I've learned that He is never far away.

Still, I have spells when I believe I can go it alone. I believe I have the strength to face whatever the world throws at me. Then comes the storm. At least now I know who to reach out to and that He will never leave me nor forsake me because He promised, and He is faithful, even when I am not. He's my Father.

Lamentations 3:22–23

Because of the LORD's great love, we are not consumed, for his compassions never fail. They are new every morning; great is your faithfulness.

Faith to Faith

YOU DON'T BELIEVE in God? Okay then, let's go with that. But you have to believe in something. There has to be a genuine belief in what happens when you leave this earth. Otherwise, you're on your own, no direction, no becoming a ghost., no hell to pay, none of that.

Maybe you believe in reincarnation and will come back as a butterfly, songbird, or some attractive, flitting thing, but what if you come back as a buzzard or a possum or a snake of some kind?

You need to think it through. You gotta know what all that involves. You have to accept that buzzards and possums also have a life cycle. They die too. So, when buzzards die, they might come back as a possum and have to die again on some country road for no reason other than they were in the path of some sleepy trucker headed to the Waffle House. It's important to ask yourself how many times you're willing to die on a road eating two-day old armadillo entrails or leftover, tossed-out fries.

Speaking of bacon, and I do speak highly of it, what if you come back as a pig? As a pig, are you destined to be bacon or ribs or, heaven forbid (lol), pickled feet? Think about fermenting in a jar or hanging from a hook for like, ever, before you come back as a tree or poison ivy or something. What exactly is it you're looking forward to being, and don't say dragonfly. When you see one, they're at the final stage of their life, so that's really not something you want to spend a lot of time wishing for, but it's your lamp. Rub it and ask whatever you want.

It does seem grossly unfair that reincarnation doesn't allow a choice. It seems that if you believe in that, then you should be able to choose which animal you could come back as, or at least, depending on how you lived, you could start out as a shark or something that has a long life, so you wouldn't have to die all the time, and even that is risky.

Then, there's this option: If you believe that you are the result of some primordial gloop that miraculously turned into a fish, then a bird, and then a monkey, then none of this matters because your science can't produce an actual god. If, in fact, evolving is an actual thing, then we are all just different levels on the food chain that would ultimately require us to consume each other at some point, depending on which catastrophic end the earth finally spins into—zombies or aliens—doesn't really matter. We're all just one giant sammich for somebody or some other life form, assuming that the original ooze splattered throughout the galaxy.

Then there's heaven, but if you don't believe in God, there's no reason to go there other than to see your family and friends again. You'd have to question how long you'd want to live with your mom and how many of the same rules would come into play: no shoes in the house, be home by ten, wear clean underwear all the time . . . Remember? I don't know, friend. I'm thinking everyday Thanksgiving is probably pretty boring if you gather and talk about what you did on earth for an eternity, and, of course, your drunk uncle isn't there, so what's the fun in that? I'd search for another solution if I were you.

Then there's the idea that nothing happens when we die and we all just turn to dust again. I've gotta think you really don't believe that because that would mean those dust bunnies under the couch are potentially a former family member or worse, so that idea doesn't have much merit in the grand scheme of things, and eternity in a vacuum cleaner doesn't seem very inviting, so, okay. Ashes to ashes—eternity is just a myth, so what else ya got?

If you actually believe that we all go to heaven if we live a good life, then there's got to be some actual rules to that. Who decides who is good and who is bad, and is that deity always available? Is he or she (it) conscious of everything you do? Can it make you promises? Can it hang a star? Can it die in your place?

If you have a different god, it may be that you would want to delve into his or her (its) character to find out if is good-natured. Can it give you blessings or lessen your load? These qualities are necessary in order to avoid mistakes. I mean, you don't want to spend eternity as a free-range chicken if you were meant to be a dust bunny. You have to know that your God doesn't make mistakes.

Your deity must be immutable and unable to break a promise. Otherwise, you're stuck with a multi-colored sticker on a Prius rather than a promise in the sky that the earth won't ever flood. It's a choice. Make it wisely.

You have to put this stuff together so you can contend for your own faith. If you don't, you'll have no converts, and your religion will suffer the fate of spirit animals or pagan gods who have been retired to movie studios rather than accepted as actual gods. There's a long list of gods out there.

Then there is the idea that we are all gods. That through some magnificent evolutionary miracle, we advance to level twenty-six in the game of Afterlife, where we obtain all knowledge and power to explore the universe without the restrictions placed on us by the human mind. That sounds pretty cool, but that also means that we are destined for an eternity of self-involvement.

I'm not sure if I want to aspire to a place where I am so self-aware that I contemplate my relationship with my (probably non-existent) spiritual navel.

Is there a hell in your future? Would hell be the loneliness associated with self-deification, or would hell be coming back as sushi for some connoisseur of uncooked aquatic life? Could it be that you spend eternity living under your descendants' couch, or do you glide around on a cloud playing a stringed instrument without the benefit of a wall of Marshall amps? Rock and roll heaven may not be all it's cut out to be.

Needless to say, you gotta know what happens after all this madness is said and done, or else you may be in for a rude awokening (or whatever tense you choose to apply to that ever-abused word that currently defines social consciousness).

These are only a few ideas that await your investigation. There are many more, but I'm going to point to the one that makes the most sense to me.

I believe in Jesus Christ. I trust that He is who He says He is. I read His book. It doesn't take long to figure out who wrote it. Now you can point and laugh and dance around the issue, or you can consider that Jesus says He is the Son of God and that He loves me enough to die for me.

He promises me He'll never leave me nor forsake me. There's comfort in that. I don't know of any other god that makes that statement or one that literally promises me heaven. I can and do trust Him because He settled that in my soul long ago. He is righteous and holy and just and good. He is sovereign, omniscient, and Almighty God, forever and ever, and that's a long time!

Mostly, though, I've learned to trust Him. That's what really matters. He is trustworthy. I trust His Word. I believe He has gone to prepare a place for me because He said so.

2 Corinthians 9:8

And God is able to make all grace abound to you, so that in all things at all times, having all that you need, you will abound in every good work.

Outliar

SOMETIMES I FIND myself in one of those moral dilemmas when I search for solutions to current issues that really aren't issues at all. They're just invented narratives that attempt to divide people. It seems to always come down to. "How do I determine who is lying?" The conclusion is always the same. I know a lie when I hear one. Liars lie, but why is that?

Discerning a lie, or a liar, has become easier as I have studied the Bible. I don't claim to have arrived by any means, but I believe that proper discernment comes from God as nothing else explains it.

Reading and studying the Scriptures has become a most convenient lie detector. Those who do not know a lie when they hear it are swayed by the liar and drawn into the lie; hence, the current situation of separation between the aberrant "thems" and the ever reliable "us."

As a young man, I was always an excellent liar, at least in my own mind. I was convinced by my own ability to convince. I outlied the liars in ways that complicated even their understanding of whatever truth I was attempting to unravel. I could so complicate a lie that even liars were hard-pressed to see through them. I assumed this was some unwritten rule of lying that a liar could not detect a lie, and that is evidently what caused them to turn to and follow other liars.

It has been my experience that liars cannot discern lies, especially their own, which is, of course, the power of them. It seems that only the unarmed will accept the word of a liar. That is not to say that we can't all be fooled, but more often than not, a lie will generally expose itself beyond a believable level.

My parents always knew, though. I never understood how they could distinguish my story from actual events. I could not accept the logic that anything blamed on my sister was nearly always received as a lie other than the fact that, of course, the princess couldn't lie, and I, being the lowly minion born of the nether regions and left on the doorstep by gypsies, would only implicate Her Highness if I was indeed spinning another terrible falsehood. I had no defense for this total acceptance of the "fairest of maiden's" word. Surely she had somehow beguiled them both. I was, therefore, convinced she was a witch or something even higher up the demon chain.

My dad always expected a lie from me. My mom would prepare a defense of the lie so that justice would prevail on the side of lesser punishment. Giving me the benefit of the doubt was her absolute superpower because, frankly, she knew too that I was lying most of the time. Her father had been an alcoholic. She was a walking lie detector. She just didn't want my father to go the distance with me. In my mind, punishment for high crimes included penalties of biblical proportion, like maybe incineration or subjection to lion's dens or some Levitical curse that only parents were allowed to deliver lest their children grow up to be lying politicians.

Luckily, my father was not a cruel man, but he believed the punishment should fit the crime, and lying was a crime of the highest order. My mother was a compassionate sort. That, and the fact that Almighty God protected me, can be the only reason I survived childhood. I was also certain that my guardian angel was inattentive and slothful, certainly not worthy of his wings.

Having been a liar, among my other horrible childhood sins, like despising my calculating and evil, bewitching sister and throwing rocks at streetlights, I developed a sense of truth, especially about liars. Funny how that works. In this case, the rule of "It takes one to know one" is definitely worth the clichéd reference.

I can, without too much difficulty, distinguish the truth from a lie but not only from my own experience. It requires that I test them against what I know to be true. I know the Bible to be true. I believe every word of it. Call me crazy.

I have no idea what others test their unsourced truths against, but I am inclined to believe that the present-day social Rumpelstiltskins gather together for a tax-exempted holiday and decide how to weave cheap moral platitudes into socially ordered philosophies, mostly intended to keep them in caviar and yacht fuel, all while serving the masses, of course. How else do you monetize political futures?

When I view the world, as it rudely demands my attention on ever-available screens and politically driven broadcasts, I bristle at the lies that flow from the mouths of those who wish to deceive their followers, which, more and more, seems to be the trend. Sometimes there are more wolves than sheep, it appears.

We need a wise and caring Shepherd, one who teaches us the path we should follow, who exercises control over His rod and His staff, thereby causing His flock to move according to His direction, and who has no fear of wolves and commands the truth because it is His own.

The spiritual battle rages, and I find that I am less prepared to engage if I'm not properly armed. I'm thankful that I can see that and am increasingly wary of any who deceive. Spiritual discernment is a necessary and ever-available weapon against lies and liars. Hebrews 4:12 says this: "For the word of God is alive and active. Sharper than any double-edged sword, it penetrates even to dividing soul and spirit, joints and marrow; it judges the thoughts and attitudes of the heart."

People who don't realize the nature of their enemy can never accept any truth because it is based on the lie that demands that there is no absolute truth. That is the first lie, to which there is this response from Jesus Himself:

John 8:47

Whoever belongs to God hears what God says. The reason you do not hear is that you do not belong to God.

Blind Stares

MY WIFE HAS one. She's perfected it. I noticed it first in the kitchen when she was instructing me on how to make green beans taste like anything but metal lathe shavings. I didn't really understand the cooking process. She just stared at me as I went about preparing everything, fumbling under the counters, preheating the oven for no apparent reason, announcing the digital readout, and affirming every five-degree increase. She just stared, never saying anything.

I, of course, took that as an affirmation that she knew that I knew everything there was to know about cooking and was quite adept at organizing and using all the various cooking implements involved in the process of creating green bean chemistry. It was nothing more than a new workshop with things and tools that do stuff. She continued to stare and never said a word.

Then came the simple instructions like, "Turn the burner on" and "Turn it down some."

It went on and on. My questions were answered in a place of absolute disbelief.

"Ham hocks in green beans does not make pork and beans."

"Yes, it does!"

"No, it doesn't" and on and on until she gave up on me and cooked the beans and stared into the pot the entire time, as if she could see through some deep space black hole. I wasn't even there.

I've learned the look and use it effectively. In my later years, mostly when younger folks want to explain the weather to me, I have actually learned to tune them out completely. I just stare. No head nod, no shoulder shrug, and no "what must you be thinking" attitude. I have learned resistance is futile. You can't teach a mute puppy an old trick.

Sometimes I stare into space and ask pointless questions because it makes them further their explanation of whatever science they claim to understand. Simple things like "Where does wind begin?" or "What starts a heartbeat?" My favorite is, "Do you believe in gravity?" They never really get that I'm literally trying to see just how many questions they will answer without a tick's hair of knowledge. That's the fun part.

It's not that I want them to fail. It's that I want them to understand that life is more than a TikTok video or Google inquiry. There is a tremendous source of wisdom that they're not tapping. That wisdom is found in the book the world has dismissed, along with its author, I'm afraid. The elder population is immediately relegated to some form of late model, green defiant, carbon-consuming imbeciles, so to relate wisdom to those who can Google it, is a completely frustrating if not futile undertaking.

Those of us who claim the Bible is the Word of God are the first to be met with an equally disturbing blind stare. It's not as practiced as our own, but it does cause a "What must he be thinking" pause in any conversation.

It has come to that. The blind stare can be directed at a cell phone. There's no need to listen to foolishness if you can appear to be preoccupied or just ignore whoever is in your immediate vicinity.

Sometimes when I really wanted to fracture the time space continuum, I just blurt out, "There won't be any cell phones in heaven!" just to see if there is any interest in the things of heaven or if I just need to go ahead and blindly stare off into space. It's impossible to gain the attention of a gamer when he is slaughtering trolls, so it doesn't matter, really.

I do wonder, though, if Jesus has a blind stare and if there are times He looks down at the earth and just stares at us without shaking His head or laughing out loud or saying anything at all because we are such a self-involved people staring at our phones and ignoring the obvious signs of a world gone deaf and dumb without so much as a nod in His direction.

There's going to come a time soon, I believe, when the woke are going to be awakened. We're all going to have to answer. I'm sure there will be a lot of protests, not to mention a lot of blind stares by those who have never paid attention to the abyss that awaits them.

Isaiah 35:5

*Then the eyes of the blind will be opened and the
ears of the deaf will be unstopped.*

The Garden of Beatin'

ONCE UPON A time, in a land pretty close to my house, there was an area referred to as the Garden. It was an older property, over-grown with brush, cabbage palms, and huge pine trees. It was as God created it, undeveloped and untouched by human bulldozers.

I was on my daily walk when I came upon a rather large, multi-colored, and unusually thick serpent. (I use walking sticks for my walks, partly because it gives me an advantage over most crea-tures, be they stray dogs or flying monkeys or well . . . any sort of demon-driven serpents.)

I spotted him at about twenty feet. He was beautifully banded red and black and yellow. He was just kinda slinkin' down the road, not particularly in a rush. I, on the other hand, decreased my speed to let him slither at his own speed. He stopped. Bad idea. So did I.

I have learned not to engage the beasts in Florida. I am fortunately well-read and have a firm grasp on all things eschatological, and I was aware that these will eventually be released onto humans around the time of the zombie apocalypse, so I am careful not to agitate them as I would prefer to be considered a friend when whichever seal is broken by whatever angel when they begin to devour us all. Shuddup. This ain't a theology lesson.

As it turns out, there's no time to recite a poem or any other form of woodsmen lore when encountering such an evil. I tried to remember it, but red touches yellow . . . something . . . something . . . is never a way to identify a venomous snake, particularly one big enough to yank you down to his level.

He turned toward me in a complete U-turn, as if he had forgotten his wallet or left a burner on in his snake pit stove. I froze. I really couldn't turn my back on him. It was as if he was daring me to continue. I stayed put. He continued coming at me.

Just when I needed my man voice, I was stricken with a choking sound from my throat that I did not recognize. It was fear, I guess, and a complete lack of testosterone, as if it had all been drained in the moment. I raised my stick high in order to try to impale the slithering assailant. I doubted it would stop the attack.

I struck with lightning-fast speed. Somewhere between the tribal dance and the little girl screaming, "Get thee behind me, Satan," I realized I had impaled the ophidian attacker with my walking stick on the first attempt. He wasn't dead, but he was trapped. Close enough!

I wasn't sure what to do, so I used the other stick to finish him off, beating and lunging, stabbing and thrusting, all of it! It wasn't a pleasant scene, but once the slaughter started, it became a matter of mercy. It was a violent but necessary ending. It appeared to be quick, but you know snakes; they tend to wiggle even after their wicked souls have slithered off to the hell from which they surely came.

I waited a few minutes to ensure the obvious. I used my sticks to move the carcass to the side of the road. This was a sure sign that would warn the others who sometimes walked their dogs past the Garden. I looked around to make sure that none of the neighbors had seen the New Balance Calypso or heard the shrill sound of fear that still echoed through the woods.

I strolled on past the neighbors' houses and around the live oak that was my quarter-mile marker, assured that no Eve would be tempted by the serpent in the Florida Orange Trees of Life today. I was also fairly sure that my man skills were still somewhat intact. I really need to work on the dance and that voice.

As it turns out, it was a venomous coral snake. The neighbors agreed that I was indeed a man among men and that it was the biggest one any of them had ever see, at least that's my story, and I'm stickin' to it.

The dogs aren't sure how to treat me now. They just kinda stare when I walk past like they are grateful that I had destroyed a natural enemy, but I think they heard the scream. I point my walking stick at them when I walk by as if to dare them to retell the story even to each other. It's our secret.

Okay, so it wasn't that big, and it wasn't a deadly coral snake, but I did kill a snake with my walking sticks. The rest are just minor details. I could have made it a dragon, and this story could have turned into an epic tale, so just count your blessings and move on. There's a lot more going on here.

John 3:14

And as Moses lifted up the serpent in the wilderness,
so must the Son of Man be lifted up, that whoever
believes in Him will have eternal life.

Big Mac

MY FIRST JOB offer upon leaving the service came from the taxi driver who took me from the Atlanta Greyhound Station to my mother's house out in the country. His name was Jim McDowell, and he made the job sound fun, exciting even. He was the owner of the cab company and seemed like a good man. I loved to drive, and the pay was immediate (cash), so I took the job until I could find something else.

All was well, and driving revelers around town was a blast. I met a lot of fun people and discovered all the best gathering places, not a terrible thing for a young man just out of the service.

A couple of weeks in, I got a call for a fare just around the corner from the taxi stand. It was personally dispatched to me by Jim McDowell himself. He told me the rider's name was "Mac" and that he was a special friend of his. I finished my sandwich and arrived at the house in about ten minutes.

As I drove up, a very lean, disheveled man stood leaning against a tree. He waved, acknowledging that he was the one who called. I called him by his name, "Mac," as he moved toward the car. He mumbled a simple "Yes."

He walked in a strange but determined manner, almost as if he had to sling each foot forward somewhat like a duck on dry land. So odd was his walk that I got out to help him into the car. He threw up his hand and told me he was fine. I smelled the liquor immediately and bowed out respectfully.

He spoke very slowly, slurring his words. It was obvious that he was intoxicated. Having encountered a few inebriated souls in my day, I politely asked him where he wanted to go. "ABC Liquor," he replied. "Yes, sir. On the way!"

From the back seat, I heard sounds, and the smell almost instantly drifted forward. Clearly, he'd had an accident, but I took no corrective action. Any friend of Jim's was a friend of mine. I would simply clean the vehicle afterward. That was just part of the job.

I drove to the liquor store and parked in the assigned handicapped space. He handed me a fifty and asked me to go in and get him a couple of pints of Old Grandad. I complied and returned, handing him the bag with his change. The additional smell of soured urine had permeated the air in my absence. I turned the a/c fan up to "high," ignoring the smell. He slurred a quiet "Thank you" and asked to be returned home.

I got him home and tried not to notice the struggle as he made his exit. He lived in a world of too drunk and brutally crippled, so who was I to judge him? It seemed to me that the one could certainly cause the other, neither balancing out the pain of whatever had started the vicious cycle. It was sad, to say the least, not to mention a lesson in slowing my own roll before things got out of hand.

There was no fare, per Jim. But Mac insisted on tipping me a twenty from the sack of elixir that would hopefully quiet his personal storm, if even for a moment. I found myself actually praying for him as he exited the car, something I didn't do often in those days.

I made my way to the carwash to clean up the back seat. Jim radioed me to return to the stand after I'd cleaned up the mess. When I arrived, he closed the door behind me and locked it so no one could interrupt our conversation. He asked if I had talked with the rider. I told him I hadn't said too much to him but that he was pretty drunk. Tears welled up in his eyes as he admitted that the fare was his own Uncle Mac. That's when he told me the story.

It seemed that Mac was a WWII veteran who had been captured and sent to a Pacific Island Prisoner of War camp. He was routinely beaten and suffered a great deal of punishment, the worst of which was being hung from a tree limb and having his Achilles tendons flayed, then cut virtually in half with a machete. That wasn't the worst punishment they offered. He endured much more, but those were the wounds that caused him the most physical suffering. However, watching his friends being brutalized was more punishing. He was the last surviving member of those who were sent to that particular camp. He had memorized each of their names and faces as they endured unspeakable horror.

Jim went on to tell me that Mac tended to start drinking about a week or so before the Memorial Day weekend. He would drink to each of his former comrades-in-arms and have conversations with each of them. It was an annual event, one Jim chose to share with me. I was both honored and overwhelmed by the fact that he would share such a personal account.

The whole story is even more horrid, the brutality immeasurable, but the memories lasted longer for Mac than any war ever has or ever could. The tears welled up in both of us as we tried to imagine what this man had lived through. We both admired his noble acts and recognized that he stood in our stead. Jim said that Mac had begged to die on quite a few occasions rather than continue to remember the horrors.

I attended Mac's funeral a couple of years later. I can say that not nearly enough flags were waved, there weren't enough shots fired in honor of him, and certainly there are still not enough stories written about the man I had come to know as "Big Mac."

I can only hope that I will be allowed to drive his chariot in heaven.

Many men like these still walk among us. They've sacrificed friends and brothers all over the world. Choose to honor them this weekend. For some, there's no such thing as a happy Memorial Day.

John 15:13

Greater love hath no man than this,
that a man lay down his life for his friends.

Joyful Noise

IT WAS IN Amsterdam that I watched an exotic dancer, aptly named Aleid, dance to a piece I knew to be written by Johann Sebastian Bach. At first, I thought it was a shameful, almost embarrassing display because I was a self-proclaimed critic of all things musical, which, of course, included dance, but then I realized that she was doing what no one else dared. She had no formal training, but her performance was engaging, somewhat of a ballet. In a word, it was mesmerizing. There was nothing seedy or edgy about the performance. She remained clothed and wore a chiffon gown that allowed her to freely express herself. It was as graceful and beautiful as the music itself. She was one with the music. It was indeed beautiful, considering the setting. She received only a smattering of applause.

I wondered how she had managed such a thing in the midst of her present surroundings. With that as my mission, I boldly invited her for a coffee in such a way as to not appear as my true self, a dusty old infantry soldier from the Georgia woods. Requesting an audience with an exotic dancer in Amsterdam is a very delicate matter, particularly in view of the clientele and the district not known for its particularly well-mannered guests.

She accepted my request for an audience, and we met the next day at a small local cafe. I had a polite conversation with her and lauded her performance She wasn't at all what you would imagine. She was well dressed and well spoken, a bit shy, and not at all impaired in any of the social graces. I was, of course, the arbiter of those traits as well, being well-educated by parents who demanded I remain in shoes and not stomp in mud puddles while wearing them.

I explored the curious nature of her work and received a piece of art that now sits high on the mantle that is my memory. She explained in some detail that she did it for her father who was a piano virtuoso and later a teacher until his death. She also said that she didn't consider what she did a performance for others. She danced because her broken heart required it. Somehow, that stayed with me even though I never saw her again. Such is the life of soldiers.

In that same vein, I had a friend in high school who was a musical prodigy, a pianist, who practiced long, almost excessive hours, but it was just what he did. We talked a lot when he would accompany me at music festivals. He made a lot of us sound better than we really were. He was beyond talented.

I asked him once how and why he continued to practice so much. He had already achieved more than most and was a recognized talent. He would go far with his current credentials. He quickly responded that his music was not so much for other people as it was to tame his own tortured soul. I remembered thinking that was pretty deep for a couple of guys hanging out after band practice. Still, it stuck with me. He was resigned to performing even though he used his talent to deal with his own demons.

In my teens, and for what has become the remainder of my life, I watched my closest friend paint from memory, scenes from his, and partly my own youth. We were about fifteen when we met. He was raised in the small town of Redan, Georgia, and moved to the bright East Atlanta lights around 1967 or 68. He has always been talented. I was fortunate enough to watch him paint during his formative years.

I have covered the walls of my home with his art because it reminds me of our friendship and his own ability to scan his memory and reproduce onto canvas, familiar country roads, deep forests, and wildlife beyond what the normal eye can see. I know why he does it. He has an artist's heart. It calms him, somehow. How else could he hold a brush so delicately and paint every feather of a bird or a pine cone you could almost pick from the tree?

These days, I watch my wife prepare the most perfect meals. She cooks them, arranges them on the plate, and sets them before me with an artist's hand. There is no one else at our table, generally, just her and me. We bow our heads before each meal and pray to the one who made the meal possible. It is to Him we present the meal together. I am privileged to enjoy the results. She, though, is the artist that combines the ingredients and hides within them spices and herbs once meant for kings. Her art is unrecognized in culinary circles, but it is highly praised in our home by any who are privileged enough to enjoy it.

In what has become my golden years, I watch a sunrise, and suddenly words just splatter onto a page. I don't do that because I particularly want to impress anyone. It's not so much a performance as it is a release. How could I possibly write about God in a world already given over to reprobate minds? For me, it is a way of offering my gratitude to the one who already possesses my soul. It is the most productive use of my time. It addresses my joy and gratitude for the things of heaven. it will, in some form or another, outlive me, so posterity is the most welcomed beneficiary.

There's a lot to be said for training, practice, study, all of that. But to truly express yourself beyond what is an established and formal path is to enjoy the freedom that accompanies any form of art. I wish I was technically better. I have no real training. I hate to misplace a comma or dangle a participle, but I practice every single day, making sure I glean from the work an offering that is appropriate to my God because I must.

You, the reader, are invited to view these offerings via this platform because I want you to not just read the words and point to my ability; rather, I want you to read them in such a way as to draw you nearer to God because I am clear that in doing so, He will draw nearer to you.

I remain encouraged because sometimes that happens. Many times, others respond to the words in private conversations or with cards or notes. Those are the times when this entire effort turns from one man's struggle to get it right into a gift of the heart, one that honors Almighty God.

It isn't for the patron, this expression of innermost joy. It is a display of what God Himself has planted in me, not by any depth of understanding of how the process works or even where the commas are inserted. Rather, it is a peeling away of what I have become as a result of what God has done in my life. These entries are my personal testimony.

Knowing from the outset that I could never improve on God's Word gives me the humility needed to express my joy in the words He has given me. My effort is always to point to heaven and praise the name of our risen Savior. For the most part, these entries are my joyful noise.

Colossians 3:23, 24

And whatsoever ye do, do it heartily, as to the Lord, and not unto men; Knowing that of the Lord ye shall receive the reward of the inheritance: for ye serve the Lord Christ.

The Patcher

I'VE SEEN THINGS, horrible things. I guess I was supposed to see them. I can't forget them, nor would I want to. They remind me of how bad the world can be for some. They give me a way to compare whatever I'm going through to things I couldn't possibly endure.

Horror leaves a scar. We shouldn't venture into places that are too stressful for our own souls without protection. I've done that. I had no cover. I've learned from it. God shields me against those visions now.

I'm sure the things I've seen don't compare to those experiences of men and women who have experienced the realities of war or suffered hardship from disease or great loss. They've seen from the inside a world others may never know. They have no way to escape the realities they've witnessed. I can't imagine the inner scars they carry. I've only skirted their encounters. I've always been far too inquisitive about these things, having endured my own trials.

I've seen the aftermath of some of those who have walked through the fire. I shouldn't have, but I was compelled to inquire. It was a choice for me but not for those who live through the collision of mind over whatever matters. I simply cannot imagine the depth of their suffering or the pain left in their souls. We hail them as survivors, but we don't treat their wounded souls. We can't possibly. That is work only God can perform.

Years ago, I befriended a man who came home from a terrible place, a place where war and destruction were an everyday reality. His job was to try to patch people up and get them moving again so that they could go back to the war and destruction. He told me the horrible accounts of some of these people. He came to realize the futility of his cause. Still, he trudged ahead. He did what he had to do.

He came home and tried to patch together a life. He fell in love, married, and went to work patching people up under better conditions. That was what made him feel the most useful. He was a compassionate warrior, bound by his skill, a righteous man who despised the suffering and pain of others.

I remember that he came home to watch his child being born in a local hospital. He cried for days afterward. We talked, but he was inconsolable. I could not reach far enough into his sorrow. He just couldn't piece together what, in his mind, was bound to fall apart. He couldn't put all the goodness of a newborn into a soul ruined by suffering. I prayed that he would endure the burden of his calling.

It appeared that he had absorbed too much of the world he saw, day after day. The horror he'd encountered, measured against the love of a child, was just too much for him to fathom. It seemed like for him, raising a child just wasn't possible, but God used his son to patch the hole in his life. He applied a father's love where only sorrow existed.

He grew to love and care deeply about his boy. I watched him instruct and tend to the only thing that ever countered the weight of his world. Eventually, he raised a good and caring young man, a musician who soothed the world around him. His father was his biggest fan. He raised him in the nurture and admonition of the Lord. He enjoyed his son despite a world he believed would tear him apart. We prayed together often. His son was always in our prayers.

Later in life, he watched his wife pass away from disease. He never shed a tear. It was a great homegoing. We talked for hours and sang her favorite hymns. The fire had forged him, it seemed. He was close to the Lord and, somehow, I was amazed by that, but I shouldn't have been. God patches people, especially His own.

He had developed a kind and delightful spirit. He had a unique perspective in that he feared only goodness because he saw it as temporary. He didn't openly grieve. He wasn't in the least callus or cold. He did the work to which he was called. His life was never really tragic because he understood his calling. He was a far better man than I. It was my privilege to know him.

My friend died today. We prayed together before he left. Only the God of heaven could release him from the wounds he suffered. He was so tender and gracious. You'd never know his pain. He was the gentlest man I've ever known. I am delighted that he is in heaven. I am sure he is among the many he'd patched, all together now, praising the Great Physician.

Having known him, I understand my own ragged soul a little more. I understand that I need to learn from the people God puts in front of me and absorb the wisdom of those who are called to His purposes...to accept that it is their race and that God will see them through. My job is to pray for their endurance and bear their burdens as much as I can. That is a great challenge and an even greater responsibility.

I know that eventually, God will patch this hole my friend has left in my soul. His memory will sting for a while, but I will remember his compassion and willingness to help others. His faithfulness will be rewarded in heaven. I intend to meet him there.

I will hear the music his son will make today as we honor his father's life. I've listened to him practice in his home for most of his life. I have often heard the sadness reverberate from his instrument, but not today. Only a practiced cellist could weave the soul of a truly compassionate and courageous man into a heart-pounding and triumphant entrance into heaven. I am sure the music from his cello will drift upward to the place of eternal peace as my friend bows before the King of kings and Lord of lords. I look forward to the presentation.

Today will be a celebration. There is great joy in the house as we prepare to leave for the memorial service. None of us have shed a tear. God Himself has patched our wounds for now. My prayer is that others will realize the gift of Jesus in the great celebration of the coming home of one of his children. Thank you, Lord, for the gift of salvation and the peace beyond understanding

Psalm 112:4–7

Even in darkness light dawns for the upright, for the gracious and compassionate and righteous man.
Good will come to him who is generous and lends freely, who conducts his affairs with justice. Surely, he will never be shaken; a righteous man will be remembered forever. He will have no fear of bad news; his heart is steadfast, trusting in the LORD.

Entrance Exam

RHONDA WAS MY niece. We weren't very close because we didn't have to be. We loved each other without all the complications of our respective lives. It was that way since she was a young girl. She moved away to Nevada, married, and had children. We kept in touch via family conversations and an occasional blip on each of our internal radar. Divorce, storms, and trials followed us both. We survived them all.

She became ill in her twenties. Her biggest enemy, diabetes, crippled her. From that came several other issues, including liver and kidney problems. Due to complications, she was forced to move home to the Atlanta area. She moved in with her mom, my sister, who cared for her during her last few years.

I got a call from my sister a few months ago, telling me Rhonda had broken four toes on her right foot. We weren't exactly sure how. Then, the next week or so, she was folding clothes and her ankle just collapsed. We never got to the point of knowing the cause, but she had rods surgically implanted in her ankle. She couldn't use that foot for eight weeks, so she was relegated to bedrest. She seemed okay, though, and my sister was able to care for her.

Then she developed pneumonia. She went back into the hospital. Due to covid, no one was allowed in to see her. After a lengthy stay, she was allowed to come back home to my sister's house. She was provided an aide to assist my sister in her care. My sister is elderly and needed the help. The aide befriended them both but quit her job, so they were left without assistance. Rhonda was still on oxygen and various apparatus that required my sister to do everything. It quickly became overwhelming.

We were helpless to do anything due to covid, helpless except to seek God's guidance and fervently pray for His will to be done. As is His custom, we were all drawn closer together during this time. Our urgent appeals on Rhonda's behalf became a place of appeals for not only her recovery but one that required our own nearly constant prayer that we know and understood the condition of our own hearts. We called in the "troops" to help us pray.

More complications required a trip back to the hospital. This time, Rhonda's oxygen and carbon dioxide readings worsened. She was delirious and had to be restrained. This was terrifying for all of us because Rhonda was such a gentle soul. She did not care for the tubes and other paraphernalia that would assist her breathing. Due to her combative behavior, she was sedated for a while, and a feeding tube was used after my sister questioned how much nutrition she was getting. We asked that they test for infection. None was found.

During the time that Rhonda was in a state of delirium, my sister would hold the phone up to her ear so she could hear me talk. She would yell "Unca! Unca!" and then sound out the words "I love you!" I cannot begin to tell you how heart-wrenching that was to hear. She wanted to make sure that I knew she loved me even in the midst of her own turmoil. It was the most important thing in her life. In this moment, as I write this. I am consumed by those words.

Rhonda got a little better and was freed from the machines for a short time. There was a moment where she was sitting up and eating green beans, her first solid food in days. We talked a bit but not very long due to her throat being sore from all the tubes. She was again allowed to go home, still bedridden but able to take nourishment.

A breathing emergency sent her back to the hospital one last time. She was sent to a rehab facility as her condition required restorative care, something my sister could not provide from home. She and my sister had become something I'll just call " mother-daughter close," so this separation caused anguish for both of them.

My wife and I sent my sister a phone so they could have video talks with each other. They shared a phone until that time. The phone should arrive today. There will be no video call as Rhonda had a catastrophic heart attack, which led to her passing in a few short days.

The last time I heard her voice, we talked about Jesus. Burdened by the machines that assisted her with breathing but still lucid and very much aware, I asked her questions to settle the matter of where she would go next. I am convinced that her responses were so clear and firm that she now resides in a place where none of the pain, suffering, or sorrow exists.

Last night, as I stared at the full moon over the lake and thought of Rhonda walking into heaven, free of all the burdens of this world, I could almost hear the words "Unca . . . Unca . . . I love you!" Only this time, they came from the place where love lives, where it first began, where Jesus resides and shouts to every one of us how much He loves us, where eternity is a reality and love is the very currency, and where the one who died for each of us welcomes us with open arms and nail-scarred hands.

Try to grab hold of this message. It comes from a broken heart and an overwhelming sense of the broken world around us. We have hope. We have promises. We are indeed destined to a place beyond this world. I know people there. I know the one who died so that I could gain entrance to His eternal kingdom. He helped me write this, and He caused you to read it.

Revelation 21:4

And God shall wipe away all tears from their eyes; and there shall be no more death, neither sorrow, nor crying, neither shall there be any more pain: for the former things are passed away.

"Whoa . . . Dude!"

I PROBABLY SHOULD KEEP this to myself, but it's important to talk about it so that other men don't suffer the same curse. The entire issue has run its course at this point. I no longer have the symptoms, and the swelling has subsided, so I'm assuming the disaster has passed.

Just to give a little background, high blood pressure is a bit of an issue for me. I see a cardiologist regularly to keep it in check. I normally take two types of medication, each affect blood pressure in a different, controlled way. I've been taking the current combination for a couple of years.

Recently, I had some issues with one of the medications. Mostly, it just made me a bit lethargic. My cardiologist decided to prescribe a different medication. That medication was called spironolactone. I never even read the label. I trusted my doctor to prescribe what he thought was necessary.

In the interim, I was having some back issues brought on by a seasonal house painting adventure. My general practitioner prescribed a fifteen-day round of prednisone, a known steroid but very effective for short-term relief. I also had a nerve block in my foot as it had been a source of problems for some time. Welcome to aging.

I began to feel better almost immediately. I didn't quite understand my sudden urge for chocolate, but I did what I had to do. Early morning bon bons and coffee became my breakfast. I had a few more at lunch and, of course, there was a variety at night. I knew

I was in deep when I began to dip the Kit-Kats into the Haagen Dazs. I just suddenly really loved the chocolate.

One night as I lay pondering the depth of my relationships and the rising temperature in the house, I felt a slight pain from a small lump in my chest area. I did a self-check as best as I knew how (I had no training) and found several lumps in both breasts. I literally screamed into my pillow and decided a mammogram would be the probable outcome. I'd never had one, so I became unusually anxious, sure that this wouldn't end well. I barely slept, and when I finally did, I dreamt about what must have been a romance novel, which scared the Fabio out of me.

The next morning, my wife asked me if anything was wrong, and I just glared at her until she left the room. She told me she was going to the grocery store, to which I responded, "FINE!" Once I heard her car start, I burst into tears. I had no idea why, but what I did know was that bon bons would fix that, so off to the kitchen I went.

I took the thermostat down to somewhere in the fifties and opened all the windows. I put my feet up on the sofa and kind of curled up. I just laid there stroking the cat, sobbing, and smashing down bon bons like there was no tomorrow. I tried to calm myself with the old Better Housekeeping magazines. I'd never actually read one, so this, too, was a first.

My breasts were killing me. I decided another self-check was in order, but this time, they were swollen, definitely enlarged, and sensitive to my touch. I called the doctor immediately and was told to come in the next morning.

The next day, after making my wife sandwiches for some odd reason, I made a beeline to the doctor's office. I rushed into the waiting room, unaware that I had worn my newest Amazon purchase, a beautifully hibiscus-printed spring mumu. I thought it would be comfortable to sleep in. I had two more coming, so I needed to wear them. I was glad there weren't many people in the waiting room, mainly because I hadn't shaved my legs and my hair was a mess. I was really anxious and clearly not myself.

The girl at the desk took one look and asked, "Mr. Drew?" I just nodded my head. The doctor saw me immediately. He asked me a few questions and examined my breasts. This was strangely exciting, but I didn't make a sound. This was the same man that examined my prostate, so I wasn't about to expose my concerns. It would have been okay if he hadn't said "Whoa, dude!" when I opened my shirt. I thought that was a bit insensitive, but we hunted together on occasion, so I let it slide.

He asked me about any change in medications, and I told him about all the changes and the increase in steroids. He gave me his diagnosis almost instantly, which was actually somewhat of a relief since he didn't schedule me for a mammogram or wink at me or anything unprofessional. He told me he would confer with my cardiologist, and they would decide on a different medication.

He explained to me that what I had was something called gynecomastia brought on by the medication and overabundance of steroids. Apparently, the meds had caused extreme hormonal changes. At my age, that was somewhat debilitating to say the least.

When I got home, I read the internet version of that condition:

"Swollen male breast tissue caused by a hormone imbalance."

Male breast tissue swells due to reduced male hormones (testosterone) or increased female hormones (estrogen). Causes include puberty, aging, medications, and health conditions that affect hormones.

I was prescribed a different medication, but the symptoms didn't go away quickly. I slept a lot better for some reason. I was quite comfortable with my condition, almost sad that there would be some decrease after a while. I thought I might miss the buxom lifestyle I had created for myself, but I decided to put all of that behind me. The chocolate most certainly had come to rest behind me.

Everything was fine until I went fishing with a buddy who commented on my sports bra. I wanted to scratch his eyes out, but he was really apologetic. I explained my condition, and he was somewhat sympathetic. He did mention that I had been squealing when I caught a fish and that I had been far too excited about the bargains I'd found at the bait and tackle store.

After one particularly nice catch, I was down on the dock removing the hook when he said, "Whoa, dude!" in about the same tone as my doctor. I looked up from the dock to catch him ogling . . . and not at my fish. Apparently, I'd had a bit of a wardrobe malfunction, causing me to flash my still enlarged pectorals. I didn't say anything, and he apologized again as we got back into the truck. There was bit of nervous laughter as we talked on the way home.

All I know is I won't be taking that stuff again. My wife is still furious that I picked through her night clothes and found some pretty comfortable undergear. She has made me absolutely swear an oath that I will never wear the yoga pants out again. Apparently, there's been some concerns and more than a little talk around town.

For the record, we will never discuss this again, so govern yourself accordingly.

MOSEY

MOSEY WAS HOMELESS, but he didn't let that define him. He was a fairly well-dressed man of the world. He wasn't crazy or a victim of any particular circumstance. Apart from his scraggly beard, most would not think him awkward at all. He was well known for his long walks around the town of Palatka, Florida. I used to see him on the back streets when I'd try to scoot around traffic. He was always pushing a shopping cart full of trash bags stuffed with what looked like clothes and an old sleeping bag. I always waved at him, and he always waved back. I did it to let him know he wasn't invisible. I'm sure he waved back to affirm that he wasn't a figment of my imagination. It was a mutually beneficial relationship.

I saw him at a public park once. Instead of just waving this particular time, I pulled into one of the parking spots there and watched him watching the world. He was a keen observer, a kindred spirit in that regard. I, too, enjoyed watching the world go by and all the people doing what people do. I got out of my truck and sort of strolled toward him, making sure I didn't startle him in any way. He offered a friendly "Hello." I introduced myself and made sure to keep my distance.

We struck up a conversation that ended up at one of the picnic tables underneath a small pavilion. He had introduced himself as "Alfred Long, but everyone calls me Mosey." We talked a while about nothing in particular. He was pleasant and engaging, even well-spoken in a charming, down-home kind of way. We openly appreciated each other's scraggly beards and laughed about how age was sneaking up on us. We talked about how difficult the process was to navigate "what with things breaking all the time and such."

After an hour or so, I told him I'd taken enough of his time and needed to be on my way, adding that it was a pleasure to finally meet him. He was gracious in his response and told me it was good to meet me too after waving back and forth so much. I believed the conversation had been light enough that we might have other meetings in the near future. I asked him if it would be okay if I prayed with him. He nodded yes, and I thanked God for our new-found friendship. When I raised my head from the prayer, there was a tear or two in Mosey's eyes. I ignored them as those are signs of reverence between him and the Lord.

I do remember that my nagging foot pain had eased during the encounter. I thought maybe I'd adjusted it or something during my stroll. It had been giving me fits since I'd turned it on the stairs. So that was good, I supposed. I drove home feeling a bit cheered up, though I didn't remember being particularly sad.

I saw Alfred a few weeks later walking past the Dairy Queen on St. Johns Avenue in Palatka. I invited him for an ice cream. He smiled a friendly smile and pushed his cart over to my truck, explaining all the way that it was way too hot to be pushing the cart. I asked him if he wanted a lift back to camp, but he said, 'No sir, it always makes me feel better when I get back to the river."

He ordered a chocolate-dipped cone, same as me. We sat on the tailgate, not talkin' much, just grown men slurpin' away, trying to beat the sun that was melting the ice cream faster than we could lick. I didn't ask him a lot questions because I didn't need to. We were friends, founding members of the Brotherhood of Scraggly

Beards; Palatka Chapter, the most exclusive club to which either of us had ever belonged.

We laughed at a stray puppy that kept trying to get in an old man's truck. His granddaughter kept trying to get him to come in, but the gran' paw would have none of that. We watched as they finished their shared banana split. Then, gran' paw gathered the plastic bowls and put them back in the empty sacks. He headed for the public trashcan, and on his way back, opened the truck door and yelled, "Get in, ya little beggar." The little girl screamed that high-pitched little girl squeal that let the world know she was ecstatic. They drove away, headed home, we presumed. We could hear her laughing a block away, still squealing and talking to her new pup. "Beggar" had found a home. Gran' paw found another mouth to feed, but his granddaughter had found a friend.

"There's still some good in the world," Ol' Mosey muttered, his white beard and mustache showing a smeared patch of misguided ice cream. "I don't want to be around when it all goes bad."

"Me neither, Mosey, me neither."

He thanked me for the ice cream and headed back down St. Johns Avenue on his way back to the river. I continued on to the Home Depot, assured that my secret stop-over would never be found out.

It wasn't long after that, I saw him again pushing his way toward Highway 19, a little farther than he normally ventured, I thought. So, I pulled over to see if he needed anything. He seemed cheerful enough but somewhat reticent to engage me.

I asked him if he'd like to have lunch with me. I told him I was dying for some Popeye's fried chicken. He said he'd never had any. I was flabbergasted. I said, "You're comin' with me then!" We hoisted his bags and cart into the bed of the truck, and off we went. I couldn't wait to see the look on his face when he bit into that spicy chicken.

He got the chicken fingers due to his dental condition, I imagined. I got the three-piece spicy white. We got a big container of rice and beans and another of coleslaw and split it so we could have seconds. We had jelly biscuits and a "big ol' orange drank." It was a chicken feast to say the least. Mosey didn't appear to be overly hungry, but we enjoyed the feast together. He was somewhat reserved but happy. I could tell he had something pressing, so I inquired as to whether or not he needed any assistance. He reached in his pocket, pulled out a crumpled note, and slid it over to me. Before he took his hand off, he made me promise that I would wait until the next morning to read the note. I agreed. We prayed together again, and again, the tears welled up. This time, both of us were affected, but I knew it was because we both knew who we were talking to.

We shook hands, and just as we were about to leave, a child ran and literally jumped into the lap of an older lady sitting beside us. The lady burst into tears and hugged that child as if she hadn't seen him in years, and that was exactly the case. We shared the moment with them. Apparently, her grandchild had been overseas with her son and daughter-in-law who were missionaries. You could cut the love and excitement with a knife. It was a beautiful moment. Apparently, she used to take him there when he was younger. It was "their" meeting place. Mom and dad came in soon after. Once again, there were hugs and smiles and a special moment when it was revealed that a new baby was on the way. Then came the love, more tears, and the grandma scream heard round the world.

We added our congratulations because it seemed like the thing to do and gathered our trays full of bones and paper trash.

"The Lord loves reconciliation. That's for sure!" said Mosey as we headed for the door.

"Indeed, He does," I replied.

I asked where I could take him, and he told me he'd have to get back to camp soon. So, I drove him all the way to the Ace Hardware. The homeless camp was very close. It was on my way, so I was happy to do it. I parked the truck and helped him with his cart and bags. He thanked me again for the wonderful meal. I pulled away, thinking that every time I engaged Ol' Mosey, something good happened. I wondered about that all the way home.

As I walked up the stairs to my house, I remembered the note. I was tempted to open it, but I'd promised my friend I'd wait until the next day, so I placed it on the bedside table next to my Bible so I'd see it first thing.

I awoke to the sound of the Amtrack train coming through. I didn't always, but this time it seemed a little louder than usual. I went out to the porch and saw that the sky was lit up like an airport tarmac. I couldn't imagine why. It appeared to be a searchlight or something. It dimmed with the disappearing train. I went back to bed and decided I'd ask at the hardware store tomorrow. I was sure someone would know. People around here paid attention to everything.

I woke up a little later than usual. I guessed it was due to the train encounter. I put on my glasses and read a few verses from Romans and a psalm or two. I prayed as always. This time, I asked God to watch out for Mosey and remove whatever was weighing him down.

Afterward, I opened the crumpled paper. It was a simple but meaningful message. It simply read "Hebrews 13:2" I knew I'd read that before, but I looked it up anyway.

"Do not forget to show hospitality to strangers, for by so doing some people have shown hospitality to angels without knowing it."

I wasn't sure what it meant, but I knew I needed to talk to Mosey. I hurried to the hardware store and asked around about the late-night lights. No one had seen it. I couldn't imagine why not. It was really bright like an explosion in the distance. I decided to find Mosey and ask some questions. He was probably still at the camp, only twenty miles or so.

I knew how to get to the homeless camp. I'd been there before. It was actually a cool little place with five or six small tents looking out toward the St. Johns River. There was a community fire pit with a few stumps around for seating. It was really quite organized as homeless camps go. It looked out over a bend in the river known locally as the Devil's Elbow. A few restaurants and gas stations were scattered about.

It wasn't a far walk back to the camp if you knew where you were going. I'd fished around there before, so I was familiar with the place. The homeless folks were in and out and friendly for the most part. They were accustomed to fishermen wandering the banks on occasion. It was peaceful there and scenic, which could be said of just about any view of the river. I headed that way, hoping to run into Mosey.

I hurried to the camp. I parked the truck at the Ace Hardware and made my way back to the river. There was only one tent, no trash bags or carts. The stumps were still there around the fire pit. Each one had a Bible sitting on it. Everything was neat and cleaned up. There was only a single, homeless man sitting on one of the stumps. I approached him casually. I only said, "Good morning." He smiled a big smile and said in a low, unencumbered drawl,

"They said you'd show up."

"Who said that?" I questioned

"You know, the angels, man . . ."

"Angels?" I started to put it all together. How could I not?

"What else did they say?" I asked.

"They told me to set out the Bibles every day and that there would be someone to come and teach from them . . . said he'd have a scraggly beard"

I sort of stammered and asked if anyone had referred to themselves as Mosey.

He said, "Yeah, but that wasn't his real name. I couldn't pronounce his real name if I tried. I think he was some kind of an ancient or somethin'. When they talked to each other, they spoke a foreign language, sounded old, one of those desert languages.

I started to do the math. Mosey Alfred Long . . . Mosey A. Long . . . I slapped my forehead and started to laugh. "Mosey Along . . . Of course!"

"Are they still here?" I asked.

"Nope. They left real early this mornin'. Prob'ly hopped a freight cause I heard the train going through town, and it was stopped for a while, changing out cars.

I asked him his name and if we could pray together. He nodded. They call me "Weed. I kinda grow on folks, and I'm liable to show up where I'm not wanted." I shook his hand and put my other on his shoulder.

I prayed out loud and asked God to watch over him. I prayed also that He would guide him in his life. I also prayed that Mosey would be safe and that his friends would finish the work they started, angels or not.

Weed started the coffee. We each grabbed a Bible and took a seat on a stump. We had a great conversation about life in general. I was able to discuss with him the perspective the Bible gives. He was immediately enthralled. We met often after that and shared with others as they would come through.

That was over twenty years ago. We started the First Traveler's Church on that very spot. We have a transient congregation that comes and goes. Our message is always that Jesus saves. We don't wander from that message very much. We don't want for anything. There is no building and no particular time for services. God always sends us people to sit on the stumps and listen to the teaching. Sometimes a few, sometimes more, but never too many.

I do most of the teaching, but Weed has taken on a lot of responsibility. I believe he's called to teach. He has such an interesting way of talking. He's curious and wants to know more. He studies a lot. The best part is, he's one of them, a true traveler, living the life.

Night services are the best. Cowboy coffee cooked over the fire is always perfect. Sister Helen from the local Baptist church brings us stuff to make sandwiches and a cooler full of water and juice. She's there almost every night and sends us one of the other ladies if she can't make it.

There are always sandwiches if you're hungry and cots if you need to rest. We have a large tent for inclement weather, but we don't leave it up. Walls seem to be too confining for travelers.

We baptize at the bend in the river. We call it Mosey's Landing. It just seemed appropriate. We sing old hymns. "Shall We Gather at the River" is sung at every service for obvious reasons. Local folks say they can hear us singing on still nights. No one complains. They know who we're working for.

We observe the Lord's Supper. Sometimes it varies from week to week, but we have it at least once a week. Transient people have a lot of questions about that. Some partake. Some don't.

The Sheriff's deputies wander back every now and again. They're never mean-spirited or imposing. One of them even sings with us sometimes. He knows all the words. He brought us a few printouts of some of the hymns from the hymnbook at his church. He spent a lot of time laminating them and brought them in a waterproof case. We hand them out at each meeting. Weed keeps them in his tent for safe keeping.

A friend named "Jammers" leads the singing most nights. He got his name from the pajama shirts he gets cheap at the Goodwill. He can really sing. Rock and roll singers burn out. That's his story.

At this point, you're probably asking yourself if I believe Mosey was an angel. I can't say for sure. All I know is God sends angels from time to time. I don't believe that ever changes. They're known to be messengers. I just know that I learned a lot from knowing him. Mostly I learned that treatin' strangers as if they might be angels is always the right thing to do.

I've never looked back. I often wonder what became of him, but I like to think he was an angel. Who's to say he wasn't? He had some pressing matters and left quickly. He said goodbye the only way he knew how. I still have the crumpled note. I keep it in my Bible.

I still see that light every once in a while. The head lamps shine through the trees just long enough to shine onto my porch before the train heads into the curve going to Palatka. The auxiliary lights tend to make the train itself appear brighter. The engineer turns them on when he's going through towns so that folks can see him better and vice versa. Not all the trains have them, but when they do, it lights up the porch, and I go out for the view and the memories. I think of it as an early sign that some travelers are on their way. Some could even be angels. Who knows? I get dressed early on those days and head up to the camp.

Like Mosey said, "There's still some good left in the' world." Sometimes you have to search for it. Sometimes it's loud and in your face., but sometimes it's back in the woods, just waiting to show itself. It comes and goes, but there's always this reminder in Matthew 18 verse 20:

"For where two or three are gathered together in my name, there am I in the midst of them."

Whether God has purposed angels or preachers or prophets or homeless men to deliver the message, we are each called to His purposes. Followers of Jesus are called to make disciples. Whoever and however that occurs is entirely the work of the Holy Spirit.

Matthew 18:10

See that you do not despise one of these little ones.
For I tell you that their angels in heaven always see
the face of my Father in heaven.

B-DAY PARTY

I HAD SEEN A broken one in Europe many years ago but wasn't particularly impressed. It seemed a good idea, but I wasn't inclined to actually install one until recently when back surgery prevented a lot of twisting and turning. I had always been a paper guy and wasn't going to be spoiled by some European water jet cleansing my bum. Besides, I wasn't about to pay a plumber to install this thing, and I was in no shape to do it myself until I had more completely recovered from the surgery.

My wife's arthritic (both hands) condition prompted me to rethink my position. So, after recommendations from friends, I ordered the bidets, one for her bathroom and one for my own; one male, one female, as God intended.

We received them via the "UPS Truck of Blessings" that frequently brought the desires of our hearts to our doorstep. We thanked the appropriate Amazon synod that deemed us worthy of such gifts once again.

The first one installed easily as I could reach the water supply lines and the controls from inside the stand-up shower. It was surprisingly simple. I tested the plumbing to ensure there were no leaks. I turned the control to "nozzle clean" and checked all the connections. Surprisingly, all was well. I mentally patted myself on the back.

I naturally assumed there would be adjustments. So, I lowered my work pants, seated myself in the appropriate position, then turned the control dial away from "Nozzle Clean" to "Rear," which seemed to be the appropriate setting, not to mention all too self-explanatory.

There was no Off/On switch, so I turned the water pressure nozzle to midway and immediately lost control of my senses or anything that might be considered comfortable. Both my legs tingled, almost burned, and sudden fear enveloped my entire body. The eye-popping reality that a firehose would be less invasive immediately caused tension just shy of rigor mortis to set in. It felt as though I had hooked this thing into a free-flowing fireplug. The stream that shot into my backside had touched a bundle of nerves never before activated. It was a perfectly accurate blast. My toes curled, my heart rate increased, and my hands started to shake for no apparent reason.

I tried to relax the flow but only succeeded in turning the shower on because that was the only knob I could reach. I immediately lost my ability to swallow, which interfered with my scream so that what came out was a high-pitched squeal that could only be described as somewhere between an approaching ambulance siren and the screams of children at a Chuck E. Cheese birthday party. I didn't recognize the scream as my own. I was uncomfortably numbed and responded in spastic convulsions that could best be described as a form of demonic possession.

I gathered my wits, which had somehow been splattered beyond recognition, and was able to turn off the shower, and in a fit of absolute necessity, I gained control of the knob to slow the invasive gusher. Naturally, I turned it the wrong way and blasted what must have been my liver into my sinuses but was somehow able to quickly adjust to the Off position.

I took a moment to slow my heart rate and gradually stood on my now weakened legs, holding onto the sink for stability. I was exhausted but somehow invigorated. I pulled up my now saturated britches and regained my composure. At least I'd be able to give my wife proper instructions so that she didn't have the same experience. That was the moment that love took over because I still have a mischievous side.

However, I fought the devil and did the right thing. He paid me back when installing her dual-jet bidet by making the installation more difficult. There was very little room between the vanity and the water supply, so it required me to use tools in my left hand, which, historically, is as useful as a stump. The process added an hour or so to the installation, but I gotterdun. I instructed my wife in detail, and as usual, she followed my instructions to a tee after reading the manual, of course.

After learning all the ins and outs, we have become accustomed to the new devices. The sight in my right eye has returned, and my voice is somewhat more manly since the initial encounter. In fact, we are becoming quite pleased with our new appliances. I would highly recommend the addition. It pays for itself in toilet tissue and septic maintenance, and it is less abrasive to those with backside sensitivities or unfamiliar invasions of privacy.

Additionally, it is nice to hear my wife sing in the morning. Sometimes I sing bass to her familiar hymns. There is music and "hallelujah moments" in our home once again. We now understand what "blessings flow" actually means (after my learning the details of the phrase "hell or high water").

Oh yeah, I can speak French now, at least I think it's French. Who knew?

Jab . . . or . . . Wakey (adapted)
Homage to L. Carroll

'Twas bringletime in the Creshirewripe
and alt amash the creatch,
There pulshered such a wickling fleap
No persleporp could breet.

The governuted paciterms
Demandered everplebes
To take the jabbershank immede
Or sumpter consequebes.

I swandered to the doctids orf
My maskle furfled swight.
In feartle subjocution
to the teleputed frite.

My sleevle rolted unkward
exporsling epidumken
To the nurshful winkled persocrat
There wraking havokracken.

The nerble went in dreep
As I shapled in the chaimt.
I slouted through the meshle
my oucher volumampt.

"It's finalied," she warmply whist
I shiveled and did swabble.
The skimpled epidorsach
Still swelpering from the jabble.

With governatal sateried,
I signafied my parcher
My photoplak in pockert now
I wampled to my cartcher.

It was this or grocerbanish,
and so in steptorcreep,
I follored all the commucasts
Obederantly sheeped.

'Twas bringletime in the Creshirewripe
and alt amash the creatch,
There pulshered such a wickling fleap
No persleporp could breet.

Southern Gospel

Y'ALL AIN'T GOTTA go! We ain't pushin' y'all into nothin' you don't wanna do! It don't work that way! You can stay down here and keep the mis'rable comp'ny. That ain't what we want for you, but y'all must see somethin' we don't! We ain't tryin' to sell anybody on heaven. We're just pointin' the way!

Sometimes it sounds like y'all see peace and happiness right around ev'ry corner. It's like y'all believe in somethin' or somebody that's gonna waltz in and make it all work, like y'all all readin' the same book or watchin' the same movie. It's almost like y'all get the same vibes about the future of the world. You're perty close, but you ain't quite nailed it down. There's definitely somethin' happenin' and, shure 'nuff, somebody's comin'!

Other times, it sounds like y'all expect ever'body to just instantly start lovin' ever'body else 'cause y'all make some radical change to the weather or discover some magic dust in a black hole you ain't quite figgered out yet. Y'all look at us like we gotta third eye when we try to point out what we believe is the truth to all that.

Here's somethin' you need to know. You ain't gonna save the planet from anything. If that was gonna happen, somebody woulda stopped all the wars by now and people wouldn't be shootin' up schools and burnin' down cities. Y'all just need to face it. You ain't got no answers. Maybe we do.

The world ain't never been safe or equal or nice or peaceful. It's always been a mess 'cause there's people in it, and people are all differnt. Some are happy but most are sad. They want what others got until they get it. Some are cruel, some are hateful, some are unjust, and some are haughty. There's a lot of complainers and a whole lotta lazy'uns, and I can tell ya there's a lotta angry ones too. As long as they're all here sharin' the same dirt, there ain't no magic pill that's gonna' make it all better.

People are differnt all over. They ain't all got a lotta good in 'em, so you ain't gonna just wash 'em up and make 'em do better. They're probly just gonna jump down into the same mud hole that you pulled 'em out of. There ain't no reason to believe otherwise.

But you ain't gotta listen. You ain't gotta go to church or read nothin'. You ain't gotta learn nothin' about heaven 'ceptin' Jesus is there. You don't need to know nothin' about hell 'ceptin' that the climate is sure to change if you don't listen.

But you don't hafta take my word for it. You can take a little piece outta this Bible here and show it to your friends cause' there's a time comin, and you don't want to be totally ignernt when you're standin' in front of your maker try'nta explain yerself.

There's more to this Jesus than you know. You might wanna listen to us before all this goes down, and it's goin' down.

John 12:48

There is a judge for the one who rejects me and does not accept my words; the very words I have spoken will condemn them at the last day.

West Wings

IT WAS DIFFICULT enough to read a map in the desert. It wasn't like you could just go down to that third mailbox or turn right at the Fletcher's tobacco barn. There was literally nothing but scrubs (small plants in the desert that never will amount to anything) and distances from the mountain towers. This was the National Training Center in the wasteland known as the Mojave Desert. It was a place where a Southern boy couldn't get a grip on the environment. There were no landmarks.

We started out from Tent City, the place where soldiers sleep in pup tents and rest from all the activity of driving around in the desert, shooting at "Russian" vehicles with what was then called MILES equipment. It's laser tag for soldiers. You shoot. They shoot you. The beeper goes off. Everyone dies at least once. It's war without all the blood and guts.

We stayed out at night some nights, sleeping on the track and eating c-rations because that's what we did. We were field hands, training officers to direct traffic, destined for a blazing hot day, stirring up dust and finding cannisters of cs (tear) gas, planted by "Op forces." We came all the way from Southeast Georgia to partake of this air that was barely breathable and this dust that made a mockery of the process. It was like gargling with peanut shells.

On this particular night we were told via radio that the next morning, there would be hot breakfast at the field kitchen, wherever that was. I didn't have a clue, being the tank commander (the guy that gets lost the fastest) and pretty well separated from our unit due to a tank chase by op forces that forced us out of our comfort zone. I decided to leave early to see if I could locate the field kitchen. I think we pulled out about 0430 or so. It was early. The desert was cold at night, so nobody was thinking, and coffee wasn't possible. We just did what we did. Onward through the dust.

My instincts told me to head west, so I decided we'd go west until we found the kitchen or ran out of fuel. We were headed as west as we could get until the sun came up, and because I was a brilliant pathfinder, I noticed the giant ball rising ahead from the desert floor, just behind the mountains. We were headed east. I decided to act like I knew exactly what I was doing. I told the driver to keep going straight.

I pulled the map out and tried desperately to find which scrub we were approaching or which tank trail led to the bacon. In an effort to orient myself, I flipped it around about ten times and tried not to look confused. A topographical map in the desert is about as useful as a one-handled wheelbarrow.

It was important to keep my reputation intact so the troops couldn't know that I was as lost as a goat in the ocean. I was only recently promoted and had failed to mention to them that I was the worst map reader since Lewis and Clark's still historically unmentioned navigator, the one before Sacagawea. His name was . . . well, no one know. He didn't make it. Gators, I think.

We drove for what seemed like hours because it was. Fuel was low. I could see the perfect storm brewing. Not being known as a particularly prayerful man at the time, mainly because of the rap-id-fire cussin', a penchant for partially distilled liquor, and a gen-erally obstinate demeanor, I did take a moment to mention to God that I didn't want myself or these fine young men to become those "dry-gulch" skeletons so often portrayed in Western movies when the water dried up. I kinda kept God on the back burner like that. It seemed fitting to at least ask Him to save us before the desert birds picked our eyes out, scorpions and sidewinding snakes decided to poison us, or whatever impending doom lay ahead, but I wasn't about to let those guys know I was driving them deeper into hell.

Just as I ended my prayer, a moment that actually sticks in my mind. I thought I heard a chopper. I didn't know why or how, but I was pretty sure I heard a chopper. I yelled into the CVC mic (communication helmet between TC and driver) for the driver to stop. He screeched to a stop, as well as a twelve-ton mortar carrier in the desert could screech, and I pulled out the old binocs and looked around for the chopper. Sure enough, it landed not a hundred yards to our faulty west. I just knew it was the field kitchen.

I contained my joy and smiled under my dust kerchief. I even laughed a little, which probably caused some alienation in heaven, but I was taking every bit of the credit for this expert map reading and timely delivery of my troops to a hot breakfast despite the timeliness of my answered prayer. I was, at this moment, the King of Scrubs (also known as privates, as they, too, would never amount to anything . . . sorry. NCO joke!).

The chopper personnel and mess hall attendants, unaware of our presence (because we were Infantry—long story) jumped out of the chopper and started to assemble a tent of sorts, then drug out some other equipment and, lo and behold, it was a field kitchen . . . THE field kitchen complete with made-to-order omelets and a fancy breakfast bar!

My first sergeant was quick to bring us over some much-needed coffee in a Mermite cannister known to keep its contents luke-warm at best. Still, it was the desert, so it was a form of coffee and much appreciated.

"You got here awfully quick, Sergeant. We only put out the coordinates a couple of hours ago."

"I know, Top. I was close."

He gave me that first sergeant look, the one your dad gives you when he knows you're lyin', but he liked me despite my rebellious nature. He was a good man and a great example. I preferred him over the imitators. He'd promoted me to buck sergeant, which was willfully negligent, but we talked a lot about the world in private, so it was an agreeable situation.

We got to eat first, so that was the highest of honors. The eggs were hot and the bacon was crispy, right there in the middle of the Mojave Desert. We call that "livin' in high cotton" where I'm from!

So, here's the thing. You've gotta get through life somehow. It's not like you can trust a map that doesn't show hills and valleys. That's why you need to learn how to read the Bible. Ask God to teach you. It is a map to a plan you will never discover on your own. It lays everything out and puts you on the right path, even when you don't know which direction to go, and at the very end, you'll go in the right direction, away from the heat. Follow Jesus. Read the book!

Whodom

Y<small>OU'VE MEASURED THE</small> distance to it. You know the breadth of it, the temperature of it, the wobble of the earth to the millimeter and the rotation of everything in orbit around it. You observe the proximity of it to every orbiting thing. You know where it will rise and at what point it will set. You've discovered the WHERE of it.

You measure its warmth and predict the distance from our world that will cause the warmth to fade. Then, with ever increasing accuracy, you predict the cool that will inevitably prevail until the cycle begins again and the warmth returns. You understand the cycle and the perpetual need of it. You understand the delicate balance. You've discovered the WHEN of it.

You realize you can never fuel it and begin to predict with some degree of accuracy, the end of its existence You shout to nothing and no one because you understand so little of it despite your relentless pursuit. You are humbled by its nature, the way it hangs in space causing everything else to rely on it. You have discovered the WONDER of it.

You begin to realize that you are just another shadow, hiding from the sun, looking for an angle and hitching a ride with the rest of us. You can't crank it, fuel it, or adjust its temperature by even one degree. Your measurements are but fool's games. Your efforts are futile. You have discovered the WHAT of it.

You realize that you must seek the WHO of it. Only then will you begin to understand the infinite power that produces and balances it in the cosmos. That is the beginning of wisdom...to accept the providence of a higher, more purposeful God to whom you will eventually bow.

Psalm 113: 2-5

Let the name of the LORD be praised, both now and forevermore.

From the rising of the sun to the place where it sets, the name of the LORD is to be praised.

The LORD is exalted over all the nations, his glory above the heavens.

Water Lou

HE WAS JUST sittin' there on the porch stairs when I went out. His tattered ol' green and yeller John Deere baseball cap gave him away. I hadn't seen him in a while, but I knew what he wanted. It was always the same thing. He just had a way.

I guess he thought I'd wanna' go fishin', but I had other stuff to do. I was makin' a whole lotta points with my wife lately, and I didn't wanna upset that apple cart.

"Let's go catch a few," he said.

I kept on walkin'. I was headin' over to the side of the house to put some salt in the water treatment system—lookin' really busy.

"I ain't got time today, Lou. I got stuff to do."

"It can wait. I got this new reel I need to test out. We don't have to be gone all day. Let's just go down to the point and throw a few." He sounded almost pitiful in a fake pleadin' kinda way.

"That's what you said last time," I said without lookin' at him.

"Yeah, but we caught a bunch. That probly won't happen again this time of year."

"I can't, man. I have to get busy on this paintin.' My wife's been after me for a month." I tried to sound frustrated.

"Well, I hear they're catchin' em over at the cut." He knew that would get my attention.

"Who told you that?" I knew my expression gave me away.

He just looked at me with that grin and pointed across the lake. I could see a couple of boats over that way. I grabbed a pole off the porch, and we headed out to the boat house. I was almost runnin'. We launched perty quick. The wind felt good on my face.

On the way over, he handed me a sausage egg and cheese biscuit, still warm. I unwrapped it from the greasy paper towel and took a bite—probably the best thing I'd ever put in my mouth.

"You get this at Memaw's?" I asked, but I already knew.

"Yep. Where else?" He knew how to drag me in. I fell for it every time.

We floated into the cut and threw up our hand at the others. They was all quiet, so we knew the fish was bitin'. I cut the engine. He handed me a green plastic mug from the thermos and poured me a cup of coffee. He made the best coffee, and it was always just right, but I could never tell my wife that.

He got on the trolling motor, and I tossed the chartreuse worm out across the pads. I was reelin' it in slow.

"We've gotta stop doin this, Lou," I said. "I've gotta lot of stuff to do back at the house and—"

KERSPLOOSH! I got hit, and it was all over but the catchin'.

We musta caught a hunert!

Fishin' with Lucifer is always good. It's like he knows right where they are. I gotta stop, though. It's startin' to be a habit . . .

2 Corinthians 11:14

And no wonder, for even Satan disguises himself as an angel of light.

Return to Sender

I'VE KNOWN MANY godly people in my life. It was clear that God had His hand on them from an early age. They experienced life in His presence and under His direction.

I've known them when they were young and watched them as they faced challenges. I've watched them as they were tempted early on. Still, they followed the Lord, always humble, serving others as if they had some special purpose beyond the norm as if they were actually called by God to do so. I wondered how they could be that committed.

Some became missionaries, some leaders in the church, others music ministers and teachers, writers, artists, and even tradesmen; all in service to God, all examples of a higher calling, prayerful, Christ-honoring people. Each of them spent their entire lives following the Lord.

I, too, was raised in the nurture and admonition of the Lord. I secretly admired these folks for their courage to face a world intent on destroying them. That must be a beautiful thing.

I wouldn't know. I am not one of those people, and there are many like me. We went the way of the world and became examples as well. We are the prodigals, those who spun out of control, strayed from the path, and did the devil's bidding, whatever you choose to call it, but we came back into the fold from places some never tread and a place from which some never return. Only a gracious God could allow that.

Yet we each stand guilty of sin before the Lord. We are somehow equally loved. We follow the same King. We are each examples of the love that shows no prejudice, a love that offers us the same hope. We are equally cleansed before a righteous and holy God. We share the inheritance made possible by the one who took our place and made us all equal at the foot of His cross.

Only a holy God could make any of us righteous. All our sins are forgiven, our slates wiped clean, our entrance into His presence assured because of what Jesus did and not by any goodness we possess. Ours is to submit ourselves to Him.

Repentance is a matter of humility and confession, no matter our station, no matter our condition. We are all sinful creatures. Our paths are all littered with stumbling blocks and enticements that challenge our commitment.

In a world obsessed with equality and justice, there is only one place where we can find forgiveness from our human condition. It doesn't matter where we've been or how far from the path we've wandered. Personally, I can only thank God for that!

The stories I could tell you . . . but I prefer the one who offers peace to the weary and hope for the sinner. God's grace is a beautiful thing. It is unmerited, unearned favor. Not one of us deserves it. Nothing can take the place of it. Yet, His love endures forever, and nothing can interfere with that.

Romans 8:38, 39

For I am persuaded, that neither death, nor life, nor angels, nor principalities, nor powers, nor things present, nor things to come, Nor height, nor depth, nor any other creature, shall be able to separate us from the love of God, which is in Christ Jesus our Lord.

Pedicles the Younger

I JUST HAD A rather intense visit with a young neurosurgeon in Jacksonville where we heard good and bad news about my rather immature spinal column. My wife and I sat facing the monitors where my spinal MRI was on screen. The doctor then proceeded to give us a complete spinal anatomy lesson that was, at the very least, informative and, at most, a lot to digest. Before he was done, it all was lost somewhere between algebra and measuring distances in cubits, but we retained what we needed and have the requisite testing referrals to move forward.

I have to admit that I was somewhat offended when he pointed out that I had small pedicles. He stopped me before I could respond by showing my size 12 New Balance sneakers. He explained that pedicles were bones that stick out from the back part of each vertebra. My wife did not crack a smile, but I heard her brain burst into uproarious laughter.

On the way home, we decided to stop and have dinner. We hadn't been out in a while, so we stopped into an excellent little Southern restaurant and partook of their chopped steak with onions, mushrooms and gravy, and a few other delicacies. I had recently received a good report concerning my sugar levels, so after dinner, we opted for the pecan pie and coffee for dessert.

All was going well until I went to take a swallow of coffee and had one of those explosive sneeze/air-cough thingies that come out of nowhere. (Well, if you live in Florida, it's some weird indigenous plant that provides pollen to the world and allergies to the populace, but I digress.) In the course of trying to inhale and induce said sneeze, I instead inhaled the coffee and a bite of the flaky pie crust and pecan filling. I can still hear the "PFAKCUHSHPLOOSH" that sounded like a pine tree cracking in a Georgia ice storm.

I was almost able to contain the outburst and virtual crop dusting that followed but not completely. The paper napkin was not exactly a quick picker-upper, so I was forced into field expediency. I picked up whatever was close. There was nothing, of course, nothing except my plague-intercepting mask and the t-shirt I was wearing. I dared not embarrass my wife, so I looked pitifully to her for assistance. I can't imagine what she saw, but the look on her face caused her to start the frantic pocketbook scramble. Lo and behold, she retrieved one of those delicate little tissuette packages that all women keep in their pocketbooks. They helped, but it was like cleaning an oil spill with a fitted sheet.

I was still coughing loudly. A heavily tattooed waitress came over and asked if I was okay and slapped me on the back in a Hulk Hogan with a folding chair kind of way and attempting to dislodge what was already displayed rather obviously in my beard and elsewhere. I'm sure that my recently discovered prepubescent pedicles were damaged in the process. Still, I felt like Doc Holliday in his lunger years.

Sips of iced tea and an experienced waitress rushing to my assistance with loads of napkins quickly quelled the panic and disruption in the room. When I finally managed a breath, you could almost hear the sigh of relief from the soccer moms and the disappointment from all the volunteer firemen who were surely about to converge on me and Heimlich me back from my dust-covered grave.

My wife went to the register and paid the check as my coughing spasm began to wane, and my blood pressure assumed its normal, elevated levels. People began to smile again, and I just sat there sipping my tea and quietly coughing into my now unsightly napkin.

As we exited the building, I could hear my wife explaining that everyone needed to excuse us. "We just found out that he has small pedicles, and he could die." She didn't say that at all, but I imagined it. I'm sure I haven't heard the end of my pedicular disorder.

The entire event could have been much worse, but I took the following away from the experience: a man's pedicles are his personal business and, there's a reason a Southern gentleman should always carry a clean handkerchief or two.

Y'all have a righteous day!

Rat Cheer

IT'S A SHAME the Southern language is being destroyed by linguists who believe it unworthy as a means of communication. As is their custom, the news anchors and producers of commercials dictate what is and isn't proper Southern English. Many of us, though, still hold to the past enough to almost mock our own drawl but also to preserve it, even if we are deemed Appalachian imbeciles by the narrators of our day. Nothing is more defining of that decline than the term "rat cheer."

To the untrained ear, the phrase evokes visions of rodents enjoying their favorite sport (for the sake of hilarity, I assume that to be a form of cheeseball) or suddenly seeing the resident house cat being broomed out of the kitchen for destroying the shredded trash bag from which they have all just eaten.

Nope! That's not what it means, not even close. Rat cheer is a location. It has and always will be as exacting as any GPS. It is a precise position that changes with the earth's rotation and the alignment of stars. It often requires a pointed finger but can never be misunderstood when your mama says it.

My grandfather would use it when we would question where the crappie was biting. "Rat cheer" would be his response. We knew that meant "This is where the fish are." They would invariably be where he was sitting on the bank or in the boat, mainly because he knew exactly what they were eating and where they were. He understood that fish schooled, so he could announce "rat cheer" without ever being wrong.

My mother, always careful to enunciate and use proper English when parenting her oft wayward children, would use the term in a mocking way when she wanted to get our full attention. It was the place we should stand when the order was given to listen or pay close attention to her instructions. "Stand rat cheer!"

In keeping with the proper designation of the terms as they related to the universe, "Rat there" was a short distance from rat cheer but not as far as "over yonder." Southern children with any proper upbringing understood exactly the distinction in these terms. There was order then, before the invasion.

As a matter of correction, though, and in keeping with some semblance of historical perspective, I knew of no one who used the word "thar" outside of Snuffy Smith and Li'l Abner, both of Sunday comic fame. These were subtle exaggerations (mockeries) of Southern language by those of the Northern persuasion who had no real understanding of how the language worked. They only intended to imitate what they heard from those they deemed hill-billies or those they assumed lacked indoor plumbing.

As popular examples, Al Capp (creator of Li'l Abner) was born in New Haven, Connecticut, so unless he was raised by a "tabacky" (?) spittin' Southern grandfather, he wouldn't have the faintest idea of Southern nuance.

Billy DeBeck (Snuffy Smith creator) was from Chicago, Illinois. In his defense, "Times a wastin'" was indeed the proper use of that phrase. Everybody used that long before it was popularized in the Sunday comics. So, kudos to him for that.

While I'm at it, the word "Sumbitch" is an often-used Northern invention, made famous by Jackie Gleeson as the "Southern" sheriff in Burt Reynold's movies, particularly *Smokey and the Bandit*. For the record, my mother, a world-renowned cussing connoisseur, used the phrase in its complete form when referring to my father all the way until her death. It is four words, thrice hyphenated and pronounced exactly as they are written.

Then, as if the mold was set, there was the *Dukes of Hazzard's*, Roscoe P. Coltrane, who became the quintessential Southern sheriff, along with a host of other law enforcement characters played by completely foreign actors. Everybody got in on this bit, so much so that commercials actually imitated Sheriff Coltrane to the point of sickening redundancy. So common was it that I named my basset hound after him. People just couldn't get enough of that Duke chasin' sheriff and his bumbling Deputy Cletus Hogg, second cousin, twice removed. Not one person in that entire cast spoke a lick of Dixie with the exception of Daisy Duke, who could have spoken Klingon, and no one would have noticed.

Andy Griffith was actually born in North Carolina, so his usage was entirely correct. Don Knotts was born in Morgantown, West Virginia, so his accent was authentic as well. Most of the rest are pretentious inventions by those who were more than likely caught in one of the proverbial Southern speed traps of South Georgia that interrupted their seasonal vacation from the frozen tundra they like to call home.

Don't get me started about the portrayal of Southern belles in movies. *Gone With the Wind's* Vivian Leigh was English. Clark Gable was from Cadiz, Ohio. Their accents were the sole invention of movie producers and linguists who made their living making colloquial butchery sound charming, a laugh a minute for those who were born and bred south of the Mason-Dixon line.

Colonel Harland Sanders (spokesman and alleged inventor of Southern fried chicken) was born in Henryville, Ohio, hardly a Southern gentleman and far removed from any Civil wartime allegiance. For the record, any self-respecting Southern colonel would have crossed sabers with anyone claiming pressure-cooked, then fried chicken was original. Those biscuits, though, surely originated in hell's kitchen; however you choose to identify that location.

I could go on about the Northern depiction of "typical" Southern people and things, but suffice to say, if (nobody says if'n) you don't understand the language, don't use it. Imitation is the highest form of flattery, but reckless mockery is well, insulting, not that we're offended. We just don't want you to think we don't notice when you try to ape the language or make scratch biscuits and sausage gravy.

If y'all need me to assist you in your attempts to speak Southern, I'll be rat cheer! Y'all come back now, y'hear?

ZOOM MEETING

JESUS: "OKAY. EVERYONE here? Good morning. It's Monday, a day I have made. Be glad and rejoice in it. I Just wanted to say—"

Jan: "Why do you always say that? Is that like a slogan or something?"

Jesus: "It's a salutation of sorts. It's actually a quote from the manual I sent you."

Fred. "What's that buzzing around you?"

Jesus: "Those are cherubs. They are a reminder that—"

Jeff: "What are they saying? It's annoying."

Jesus: "Holy. Holy. Holy—"

Jeff: "I heard you the first time!"

Deb "What are you wearing? I thought we should all try to look at least a little professional.

Jesus: "It's a robe."

Debbie: "I thought so."

Jesus: "So, I gathered you here to tell you—"

Jan: "I read most of your report—complicated . . . Way too wordy."

Jesus: "Which part?"

Jan: "Genesis through, well, all of it, especially about wages."

Jesus: "Do you mean the wages of sin?"

Jan: "Yes, I hope we are all paid equally."

Jesus: "Oh, you will be unless—"

Bruce: "Sorry I'm late, I was just seeing my partner off."

Jesus: "About that . . . we should talk."

Tamara: "Are we going to talk about this pandemic or not? I have a lot on my plate!"

Jesus: "It'll be cleared soon enough!"

Tamara: "Sometimes it's too much. The kids are home. Dave is working in the next room . . ."

Jesus: "Perhaps this time together will be good for your family."

Tamara: "At this rate, it'll be good for the lawyers."

Jesus: "So, I wanted to . . . This is going to get a lot worse. Moving forward, it will be necessary to—"

Fred: "Sorry . . . Be right back. The dog wants in."

Sheila: "'I'm here. What did I miss?"

Jan: "We were talking about wages."

Jesus: "No. We are talking about . . . We're closing—"

Fred: "Wait! What?"

Jesus: "Well, it's almost time to bring my children home."

Debbie: "You're kidding. In the middle of a pandemic?"

Jan: "We are all home, or did you miss that part?"

Jesus: "Yes, I know, but I'm talking about an eternal home . . . in the clouds."

Tamara "I don't trust the cloud security. We need to talk about that. I.T. says we've been hacked before…and"

Jesus: "Not that cloud."

Jeff: "So, are we all gonna be terminated . . . on what day? I need to put out a few fires."

Jesus: "I can't answer that, Jeff. I don't know the day or the hour. Only my Father knows that."

Tamara: "We're being relocated to the Home Office? I can't move. I've got kids and . . ."

Jesus: "None of you will be making the trip."

Bruce: "So, we're done then?"

Jesus: "Yes. There was no other way."

Jan: "But we were told there would be a grace period before the end so we could at least get our resumes out there."

Jesus: "There was. You didn't listen—"

Tamara: "Will there be severance?"

Jesus: "More than you could ever imagine."

Fred: "Did anyone hear a trumpet sound or something?"

Jeff: "I heard shouting. My neighbors are probably at it again."

Debbie: "Where's my daughter? She was just here . . ."

Jan: "I can't find any of my mom's texts. I hate Messenger updates."

Bruce: "I probably need a new router or something. Did anyone else lose the meeting?"

Tamara: "Jesus, I've lost my connection. Can anyone else hear Him?"

Fred: "I think we're having an earthquake. I've lost the meeting."

1 Thessalonians 4:16–18

For the Lord himself will come down from heaven, with a loud command, with the voice of the archangel and with the trumpet call of God, and the dead in Christ will rise first. After that, we who are still alive and are left will be caught up together with them in the clouds to meet the Lord in the air. And so we will be with the Lord forever. Therefore encourage one another with these words.

Counter Love

I'M MOST FORTUNATE in my life to have a few close friends. I'd take a bullet for any of them. I don't say that to them out loud. It is just that I'd rather be in the great beyond waiting on them rather than suffer a miserable, failing world without them.

A few of us have been through a lot together. I love them. They know that because I tell them, maybe not in words, but if they need something, anything, and I have the ability to give it to them, it's just a matter of the exchange. What's mine is theirs. I believe they feel the same way when it gets down to it. They probably wouldn't admit it because we joke a lot, but their love is just a given.

I have one special friend, though, who I've known for quite a few years. The goodness shown to me by this one friend is more than could be brought by an entire band of Christmas angels. It isn't something we talk about, yet it has been so glaringly important to me that I feel I must share the blessing. Pardon my public show of affection.

Each morning, I am blessed with her recurring gift. I cannot imagine a world without her daily input. She makes the world a better place, one that is survivable in this place of condemnation, this unholy, irresponsible place where people exist only to harm each other.

If you are reading this, you should know that this friend will make herself available to you as well. Being without her would be a terrible loss, but she has enough love to go around. I'm not sure that I could continue to navigate this world without her.

You're always there for me, available, there on the counter, so I don't forget, offering spoonful after spoonful of your beautiful, fibrous soul. I thought it time to publicly announce my love for you. I feel almost selfish not sharing you with the rest of the world before now.

I am forever indebted to you, Meta. You are the song that keeps on singing. You bring happiness to my day. You keep me moving toward the light. How could I live without you? I'll never let you go! That's a promise!

No, not that Meta. Don't be silly.

Thank you for all you do, Metamucil.

You are a breath of fresh air, the wind beneath my bidet. You soften the blow. You are the perfect mix tape when my soul needs to be refreshed.

I am indebted to you forever!

—Stan

The Dragonian Effect

SO, HERE'S WHAT happened. It was bats, alright, vampire bats . . . people who turn into bats. Yeah, those! Y'all just need to put two and two together.

The backstory is that there's not a lot of vampires in China. That's because dragons eat 'em. When someone gets neck-bit over there (or under there since we know you can dig down and go straight to China), they turn into a bat just like over here, only down there, they don't last long because dragons eat 'em by the thousands.

The Wuhan wet market has always been a feeding ground for vampires. It keeps 'em from sucking the blood out of people. Now, vampires really don't like Chinese except maybe the General Tso's chicken. I'm with 'em on that, but that's about all. I don't engage them, so they pretty much leave me alone. I treat 'em like gators. It's a good practice not to encourage 'em.

So, one of the Chinese folks by the name of Chu developed a virus and went to work in the market anyway. He was working late trying to get all the dogs and octopi ready for the annual Vampire Week, which is kinda like Bike Week over here. He was neck-bit while trying to hang the decorative entrails before the vampire gangs all swooped in, but they came earlier than expected. It was actually an accident because the vampires never expected a human to be in the middle of all the entrails.

It was his own fault because everybody knows drunken vampires will eat anything unless it's got garlic in it, but y'all already knew that.

Once he was bitten, naturally, there was a feeding frenzy like there would be if you set out a pan of sausage biscuits at a South Georgia funeral reception. It was just like that.

So, a bunch of vampires had a taste of Chu's blood and went about the business of partying till the sun came up. Well, almost, because they kinda spontaneously combust when the sun comes up, but you already knew that too.

Now the dragons know not to come to these things, but they're not like vampires, and they don't exactly wait for an invitation. So, the dragons did what dragons do and flame-broiled the bats from above for a quick and tasty meal. They didn't know that the vampire bats were really people and, as you know, people tend to kill dragons, and it always ends up the same: arrow through heart, dead dragon, and big village barbecue; dragon ribs and tater salad every single time. Watch any vampire movie for cryin' out loud!

But this one dragon, the one they called "Vlad," not knowing that the bats were really people, ate one of the vampire bats that sucked Chu's blood, who, you'll remember, had a virus, the source of which no one really knew, but Chu was known to partake of a lot of not necessarily cooked seafood. Think urchin-tentacle sushi.

That's where it started, right there in Wuhan, but not at some Bill Gates satanic temple and pandemic research lab or because someone ate a bat or any of that other stuff. In fact, it was just the opposite. A drunken vampire bat neck-bit a Chinese man. Then, a dragon ate an infected bat. It spread from there. The earth rotates. People suck. Things happen.

After the impromptu bat feast at the market, the dragons all headed back to Europe with Vlad in tow, now sick with fever and just wanting to be home to recover.

At this point, you must know that breathing fire is a reflex action for dragons. When they have a cough, they don't breathe fire; they just spread germs, lots and lots of germs, just like us. It is physically impossible for them to cough into their sleeves because they don't wear sleeves or have elbows . . . or manners.

Now, as a matter of explanation, Vlad had a bit of asthma as a child and, had it not been for his inhaler, he may not have been able to make the trip. The rest of the gang would have remained, and the virus would have stayed in China. But he manned up and coughed and wheezed all the way home, his inhaler his only relief. He wasn't aware that he was spreading the Chu virus all over Europe. As history will surely place blame, he will forever be known as Vlad the Inhaler.

Mister Chu will go down in history as the first victim of what will come to be known as the Corona-Not-New (CNN) virus.

People everywhere will forever associate his name, Ah Chu, with cold and flu symptoms. You may even hear the German blessing "Gesundheit" following the mention of his name, which means, "Go away, vampires" to all of you not fluent in the language.

And that's really the true story of how we all had to go indoors and watch the news and binge television we wouldn't otherwise watch because we were told that the options were only certain death and calamity beyond anything we'd ever encountered. Clear-thinking people gathered supplies knowing that large amounts of toilet paper set on fire would make the dragons think they'd already torched the homes of those who lit fires in their yards.

You might as well believe that's how it happened 'cause it's as good of a conspiracy theory as you'll read on the internet today. It's full of partial facts, popular movie comparisons, and other mysterious information you already know to be true. There are even facts that I'm sure if a news anchor repeated them, they would be believed by at least 26 percent of the population of Nova Scotia. If there were charts and graphs associated with the presentation, I'm sure there would be dragon sightings and stories of vampires swooping down and sucking the life out of the common folk.

Now get out there and flatten that curve or whatever you think you're doing to keep the world safe. Just don't mess with any dragons because, well, they're dragons, and don't feed the dang bats because at least 16.7 percent of them are people!

The WHO and research scientists at Kimberly Clark in association with Georgia Pacific have ordered that we all set our yard on fire with toilet paper whenever the vampire alarm is sounded. We should all wash our hands in garlic and wasp spray. The CDC has mandated that we all wear body armor because, historically, dragons fear knights.

Also, if you suspect any of your friends or neighbors are turning into bats, call the vampire hotline at 1-800-VAMPIRE. As usual, you're welcome.

Alec•kazam!

The saloon got deathly silent
As the doors swung open wide.
He looked around the room,
His wooden pistol by his side.

No one dared to catch his gaze
Because it didn't matter.
That gun had killed before without his help.
So, they all scattered

One remained who had no fear.
He'd seen the man before.
He knew at once the time had come
To settle an old score.

He remembered with a searing pain
The night the stranger came
and took him and his innocence.
He'd never been the same.

He stood and faced the 'slinger
That recognized his face.
He started for his pistol
But quickly lost the race.

It's there the bullet took him
Right between the eyes.
He collapsed off in the corner.
No one was surprised.

The Baldwin Brothers heard the shot
and burst into the room.
Stephen was the first to ask,
"Did Aleck's gun go boom?"

"It was an accident!" he cried.
They'd heard that song before.
But there he was, the Canteen boy,
Now dead upon the floor.

The ladies all began to wail,
Then screamed together, "Why?"
"He was just a scout," they said.
"He'd never hurt a fly."

"I did not shoot, as you can see.
My wooden gun is magic.
It shoots itself. I'm not to blame.
This is just terribly tragic."

His brothers circled round him
and backed him from the fray.
Their pistols drawn, they mounted up
And left without delay.

They rode to where they knew
They'd find some shelter from the ire.
Where else but Hollywood
Are magic guns allowed to fire?

Still, there are no questions
Why a movie prop was loaded.
Or how or why a magic bullet
Suddenly exploded.

So here the legend ends
With Canteen boy deep in his grave.
But Aleck rides again.
Another actor has been saved.

The whole affair will disappear
As quickly as it starts
As long as all the actors
Read their scripts and play their parts.

I'm sure this poem will go the way
Of narrative detention.
Such is the way of magic guns
that draw too much attention.

St. Charles Ave.

HE CONVERTED SO many to his cause. He was the picture of love, humility, and goodness. He was eloquent, perfectly poised, and socially aware. He was a gift to the world. Surely God would have mercy on us all. After all, He sent us Reverend Charles.

His hair was perfectly coiffed, his teeth as white as his unblemished heart. He literally oozed redemption. You could feel it in your bones when he smiled. He was, indeed, an ambassador of heaven, sent by God to teach us all how to live our best life.

He preached a word that brought others healing and prosperity. At least that was what he said. He never used bad words like the other preachers. Repentance wasn't necessary, nor was sin a cause for punishment. Just send your money into Reverend Charles. He'd do the rest. He was, after all, gifted with the Spirit. In Jesus's name, hallelujah, amen!

He went to be with the Lord on a Sunday. How fitting! Entering heaven on the Lord's Day just seemed appropriate. All the celebrities showed up for his send-off. He will be remembered. The star on the sidewalk will ensure that, especially since they renamed the street in front of the church after him, and by the throngs who read his books and wore his twelve-dollar prayer bracelet when they prayed (plus shipping and handling, of course.) He was indeed an example to us all.

It was a big deal when he finally passed. All of heaven was abuzz with anticipation. They had practiced for weeks. The pearly gates were opened wide. It appeared that he would be greeted by the

Savior himself. He was hoisted onto his chariot and escorted to the gate by angels dressed in flowing white robes. Flutes and harps and a hundred violins followed. The music filled the streets. It was glorious!

Angel trumpeters and a great chorus announced his presence. Rose petals tossed about on the path presented a beautiful fragrance and a picture of all the respect due him. Not since Elijah entered eternity had there been such commotion in heaven.

Just short of the entrance, he saw through the gates into a great hall that a glimpse into heaven was worth the price of admission, and he had certainly paid his dues. And there, on the throne of grace was Jesus, the Christ, the Messiah, the Savior of the world, the one to whom he owed his very life and ministry. He at least wanted to shake His hand.

From the gate, he peered down the streets at the mansions and tried to make out which one would be his home for eternity. Each one had a name. There was John and Mark and Steven, Abraham, Moses, and Paul. Everyone was here. He couldn't wait to meet them all.

He was welcomed by an angel dressed in a kind of greyish hoodie who pointed the way around the path to a side road. He could still see Jesus, but He neither stood nor turned to face him. He found that odd considering all the pomp and circumstance, but he continued to follow his escort. He'd learn the ropes quickly. He always did. He was sure he was in the right place. Home . . . Finally!

As his chariot made its way down the road, he could barely make out the sign in the distance. It was a marker of sorts just behind the street where he'd seen the homes of the prophets and apostles. He could just make out the word "Charles," so he presumed this would be his new home. It looked like it was still under construction. It looked as if it was an excavation site. The dirt was piled high in a large circle revealing what appeared to be a deep pit. The sign he had seen that bore his name was not what he thought. It didn't say "Charles." It actually read "Charlatans."

That's when he smelled the smoke and heard the crackling from the fire below. The screams were faint but couldn't be ignored. The closer he got, the more the reality set in.

He looked toward the throne, which was no longer in his view. He shouted aloud so all of heaven could hear him. "How can this be? Lord, did I not prophesy in your name and in your name drive out demons and, in your name, perform many miracles?"

The music stopped; the chorus ceased. There was silence in heaven. Without hesitation, a voice like thunder responded just as He said He would.

"I never knew you; depart from me, you worker of lawlessness."

Those words echo throughout eternity. They are words you don't want to hear.

Jeremiah 23:16

Thus says the Lord of hosts: "Do not listen to the words of the prophets who prophesy to you, filling you with vain hopes. They speak visions of their own minds, not from the mouth of the Lord."

Sacrament of the Smashed Nanners

FOR THOSE OF you who don't know, we are a family of devout Puddinites. There aren't many of us left. We are a small but humble congregation of worshipers.

Today is a religious holiday at for us. We are a particularly dedicated sect determined to continue the traditions of our Southern ancestors.

We have guests for the holidays, the much-revered Brother Roy and Sister Tammy Jones who have made the pilgrimage to the Holy City of Crescent in order to offer their bodies as vessels to the annual Rite of Consumption.

The day begins with fishing. This exercise builds focus and patience for the requisite submission to Our Lady of Delightful Creations.

According to the time-honored traditions of the Church of the Consumption, the requisite shoulder meat was smoked using the applewood pellets by the ordained minister of porcine delivery, Brother Stan of our sister church, the Church of the Sunrise Smokehouse.

The offering was presented with the proper incantations and blessings and a light painting of holy sauce. The elements, large knives, and other piercing implements were distributed amongst the parishioners with the associated side dishes, including the Coleslaw of Temptation and The Consecrated and pickled asparagus.

The appropriate amounts of extracts and spices are then gathered and combined in secret as the tradition requires. Prayers and offerings will, of course, be made at the dining altar once the pudding aroma begins to cause trance-like utterings in the language of angels.

Following the Devouring of the Purified Meat and cooking of the miracle pudding, the Sanctified Pudding Mother, Sister Lynn of Delicious Endeavors (so ordained by the Council of Partakers of the Elongated Fruit from the Tree of Goodness) will properly adorn the pudding with the white Meringue of Goodness.

The Rite of the Spooning of the Heavenly Nanner Pudding will begin promptly at 6:30 p.m. Those who prefer their pudding warm will indulge first. All others will have to wait for the Monks of the Refigeratory to perform their reading of the Book of Recipes in accordance with their sacred vows.

The services will begin after the appropriate hymns are sung (i.e., "Dixie, " "Oh Susanna," and, of course, "Old Abner's Shoes, the last being an effort to root out those of the Northern persuasion").

As usual, there will be no preaching, and the Implements of Consumption will distribute to the congregants in order of appearance. Tablespoons are allowed. Absolutely no raucous behavior or banging of bowls will be permitted!

At the point of actual consumption, there will be complete and reverent silence until such time as the bowls are emptied, whereupon seconds will be administered by the Steward of Suffering.

The sacrament will end at the Belching Altar, otherwise known as the Sofa of Comfort and Joy. The rite is now complete until such time as the Order declares their next meeting.

"Nanner Pudding is to the soul what Custer was to the plants at Little Big Horn."

Signals

MY MOTHER AND I had a mutual "gift" that no one else knew about...not even family members. We could each raise an eyebrow independently of the other. She her right brow, mine, my left. I still possess this talent but no longer use it to communicate in the way that we did.

We used this unique talent to signal each other when we knew we must try to wade through the next few minutes of life without letting on that my sister's drama was overdone, my dad's sermon was unnecessary or that the story my grandfather was telling for the umpteenth time, was as true as it was any of those other times with the exception of the new parts...

My mother was a World Champion cynic...but you'd never know it because of her other talent, that being the most perfectly nuanced subtlety known to humankind. The level at which she performed these signals was masterful. My father recognized some of them but they infuriated him. She knew that. It was part of her charm... and her arsenal...but the eyebrow raise was ours.

I learned the other traits from her, not knowing that performing them was an act of self-approval. Performing these nuanced gestures meant that you understood something that wasn't just right, and you used a slightly physical act to tell yourself that whatever it was, didn't pass the smell test. If not performed correctly, the secret acts would be obvious to others. That's the beauty of them. Their misuse is the perfect crime.

My dad on the other hand, was an eternal pragmatist. The only signal he had was a stare over the top of his glasses that could stop any crime I was about to commit, before it was actually perpetrated. He would shake that huge ham sized "Honeymooner" fist at me, just in case, to warn me of the severe consequences if I continued.

I stood on the deck this morning, looking out over the water, I was thinking about my mom and which side of heaven she was on...because I knew my dad would most certainly be on the other side...They weren't exactly friends in the end and I was sure they would still need to be separated in heaven. I kinda' laughed at my own absurd thought and shook my head at the terrible theological picture that thought presented...but as I stared up into heaven, my eyebrow raised without my even knowing it...

Then, looking in the other direction, I intentionally shook my fist at my dad, mimicking his Jackie Gleason styled "To the moon" gesture...I was sure he saw that and I was almost certain he did it back.

I was assured as well that my dad didn't notice the eyebrow...nor did either of them notice the tears that welled up as I squinted into the sun.

Their birthdays are days apart...My dad's is the first and my mom's the fifth of August.

I imagined a stroll through heaven to visit each of them on their respective birthdays and how it probably took those three days in between to get from one mansion to the other.

Happy Birthday, y'all! I still miss you both...I'll be visiting as soon as the Lord allows! Y'all keep the porches swept!!

Ephesians 6:1-10

Children, obey your parents in the Lord, for this is right. "Honor your father and mother"—which is the first command-ment with a promise— "so that it may go well with you and that you may enjoy long life on the earth."

Stealing Second

NOEL FRINGE WAS, hands down, the best baseball player the world had seen in years. He consistently hit above .370 and did that for several years, surpassing even the great Ty Cobb. He always won the batting title (consecutively for the last four years.) It was becoming a given. He was considered the best batter since Aunt Jemimah's Pancake Mix. Everyone knew it.

He was an exceptional pitcher as well, with a wicked 100-plus mph fastball and a curve that would drop like a boulder. On top of that, he had a freakish change-up that took years to perfect. No one could hit him with consistency. No one.

One day, while taking batting practice, his bat splintered and flew toward the stands. A piece hit a young, inattentive ball boy in the side of the head, killing him instantly. The world was shocked and saddened. Everyone associated with the game mourned the loss of a young fan doing nothing more than having the time of his life, including Noel Fringe.

It really wasn't his fault. It was part of the game. He'd missed the pitch, really. The bat splintered and flew beyond the dugout, taking an odd angle off the glove of the first baseman. He had no control over that. It was an act of God. Even his therapist told him that.

That was the first of nine unrelated instances. A total of four infielders: one pitcher, two coaches, one umpire, and the one ball boy were killed or badly hurt during a Fringe at bat. It was uncanny and remarkable . . . freak accidents all, to say the least. People started to watch baseball just to see if it would happen again.

After each accident, the bat was inspected, the pieces forensically examined, the swing broken down to its most exacting slow-motion features, the trajectory measured—everything was put under the microscope. Nothing could be found. Each fractured piece of the bats was relegated to events not consistent with the norm. It almost seemed supernatural, as if it were predestined by some unseen source.

Pitchers started to throw at him rather than risk injury. When they did that, he would rush the mound and try to deliver his own form of justice. That was the game. He would not be intimidated.

If he was pitching, he would retaliate with a fastball to the upper torso. He was warned and removed from the game anytime he retaliated, which was every time he was hit by a pitch. It seemed like a fair exchange. Each side understood the rules.

But it seemed the rules were the rules until Fringe was at bat. Then everything changed. He was suddenly considered dangerous and unmanageable. The League started to fine him and demanded he not retaliate. The League Rules Committee convened and actually wrote a new rule they called the "Fringe Retaliation Rule." He was no longer allowed to rush the pitcher when he was hit by a pitch. If he did retaliate in any way, he would lose the privilege of playing the game he loved, forever.

So, he stood, never flinching, never budging an inch, taking whatever was thrown at him, and obeying the absurd rule made to keep him from playing his best. His batting average dropped. He was no longer a fan favorite. He suffered a lot of broken bones and continued to be a target until he was just a shadow of his former self.

One day, as he went up to bat, he pointed to the first base side. Not since Babe Ruth had anyone predicted a home run, but that wasn't his effort. He pointed to the pitcher as well.

The pitch came, a high and tight fastball, as expected. He stepped backward and hit the ball below the middle of the bat, splintering it immediately. The pieces flew in two directions, piercing the first base umpire and the pitcher at the same time. It was a horrible scene, and Fringe was tossed for no other reason than coincidence.

This time, though, they took his shattered bat. He was done, excommunicated, banished!

For the moment, the world was a better place; at least, it was safer. He'd become a jinx, something baseball couldn't embrace. Even the locker room turned on him. He was ostracized. He almost accepted it . . . almost.

He was summarily retired from the game he loved, but he wanted to give back in a way that would improve the game. He decided to make a less dangerous, lightweight, and indestructible bat so that the out-of-control incidents could never happen again.

He met with his longtime engineering friend and college roommate, Max Schall, who immediately started a research and development company. Together, they embarked on a project to improve bat safety.

It was a tedious process, selecting wood and improving bats beyond their limits while conforming them to established weights and measures., Even more difficult was getting the League to accept any material changes since Noel was the only one to have ever caused harm beyond the occasional accident.

Using his engineering expertise, Max Schall discovered that the bats could be made with denser wood and still remain lightweight. He used a knotty pine gathered from Georgia-grown pine trees that had uniquely dispersed multiple levels of condensed knots. These were carefully formed and treated with an almost impenetrable "graphene." Each bat, now known as the "knot bat," were made to conform to league specifications. The Max Schall Company's knot bats quickly became the League's standard and were considered to be the best ever produced. Not a single one ever broke or splintered. Noel Fringe personally tested each one.

The introduction of the bats made the baseball world a safer place. The bat manufacturing plant was moved to China due to the availability of the wood now genetically engineered and grown specifically for the purpose of making baseball bats.

After a few years of unprecedented safe usage, the League gathered to honor the two innovators for their mutual invention and subsequent determination to make baseball safe for fans and players alike. The Schall Company knot bats were the epitome of excellence. Their success marked the beginning of a new and safer game day experience. It was time to celebrate that achievement.

Everyone was there. The commissioner spoke. Max and Noel were photographed and interviewed dozens of times for posterity. It was all about the game and the passage of time. They made Bat Day a part of the ceremony. Every fan in attendance received a Schall bat. It appeared that Noel Fringe had overcome the demons.

At the Opening Day ceremony, the first pitch was thrown by a former Yankee pitcher nicknamed "Chaw McChunk" for his oft bubblegum-filled cheek. He had once hit Noel with a better than average fastball in the right hand, requiring surgery and months of therapy to recover. The two former opponents smiled at each other as Noel limped up to the plate, his frame clearly bent from the years of undeserved punishment. He pointed at McChunk. They both laughed and remembered that historic day.

The pitch came in slowly, as expected. After all, it was just for the cameras. Noel saw it taking a perfect arc and stepped into it. His swing was still perfect, but just as the ball met the bat, with every lens pointed at the historic moment, the bat shattered into at least a dozen pieces, one of them literally disintegrating the mound, along with McChunk. A corporate gasp went up from the crowd.

The explosion from the splintered bat took out the League boxes along with a bevy of political wannabes doing cameos for the constituents at home, making their usual cases for reelection. The cameras caught only the white light that flashed from the loaded bat. Needless to say, there was no joy in Mudville.

The story goes that Noel Fringe had left a note about the special bat. He said it was the only one in existence with that kind of unique inner core. He'd bought the technology from the Chinese as part of the Schall Company move. Each piece was a miniaturized guided missile programmed to do exactly what it did.

A piece of the bat was found two blocks away from the now abandoned stadium. It was signed by the greatest baseball player who ever lived and died for what he believed was a cause worth fighting. It seems that the "Fringe Retaliation Rule" was overruled in the end. Noel Fringe no longer suffered. He died in the blast. Somehow, no fans were harmed on the final play.

The remaining piece of bat survived the ensuing media circus and ultimately found its way to Cooperstown, the perfect photo-op for those who once loved the game.

There, forever enshrined behind the glass that displays the last souvenir from the last baseball game ever played, hangs a piece of the last bat ever swung, inscribed by the manufacturer and signed by the best player ever to play the game.

"Schall Knot – N. Fringe."

Here's What Matters

It matters that you don't get sucked into ideas or conversations that don't matter.

It matters that you start your day thinking on the things that do matter, asking God for direction, and seeking His purpose for your life.

It matters that you love people even when you don't understand them.

It matters that you listen before you exercise your right to shout down others.

It matters that you respond to people in love no matter how much they hate you.

It matters that you know the Judge when judgment comes.

It matters that love matters, and it matters that God loves you enough to send His Son to die for you.

It matters that you spend some time thinking about that. It matters that you consider where you will spend eternity.

Time matters. This moment matters. Take a few moments to consider your options.

In the matter of what matters, you matter. Your life matters. Love matters. Eternity matters. Jesus matters.

1 Timothy 2:5–6

For there is one God and one mediator between God and mankind, the man Christ Jesus, who gave himself as a ransom for all people.

Common Man

I'M AN AVERAGE guy, no better, no smarter, no more eloquent in my speech, not overly shrewd, and certainly not more knowledgeable than others of my common upbringing. I seek no power beyond that which affords me, nor do I seek to be the master of any other man.

In the world, I have only my experiences and limited vocabulary to explain myself. I fear no man, no situation, and certainly no government authority that demands my compliance to the will of other men.

That is not who I am before God, nor will I kneel to any other king. I am the protector of my family and a dedicated friend to anyone who accepts my friendship. I am fair and just in my dealings with others.

I am unaffected by the charges made against me by horse thieves and traitors. My values are not conditioned on any man's lack of them, nor is there a referendum on my allegiance.

You may bend the world around me to what you believe to be the best suited for your struggle, but you will not cause me to accept what I know to be immoral, illegal, or overly intrusive.

I have no enemies to speak of beyond those who choose that position. I am a protected species. My God assures me of that. No other assurances matter to me. I am under no obligation to adopt your opinion as my own.

You haven't heard from me in a while, but I'm still here; no less the man God intended and certainly still trusted to defend my homeland and my personal boundaries.

I am not faint of heart, nor am I responsible for your condition, however failing it has become. I am responsible for myself and not dependent on your wealth, opinion, or idea of how I should make your life better.

My intention is to assist those who cannot help themselves by whatever means I have available. It is not to serve the lazy nor the ever-mounting government pettifoggers. I will not be intimidated by their willful efforts to steal what I have earned.

I am every common man who seeks a higher purpose. I answer to the God of heaven and seek after His will rather than my own. I will not beg your pardon. I am a servant of the King!

Micah 6:8

He hath shewed thee, O man, what is good; and what doth the Lord require of thee, but to do justly, and to love mercy, and to walk humbly with thy God?

An Eye for a Tooth

SOMEWHERE IN THE mid-eighties, I had an accident that caused me to get plastic teeth while still young enough to navigate life without a scooter or an optometrist. The initial accident occurred at a great height and involved a frayed but trusted rope of substantial strength but not strong enough to prevent me from bouncing off several protruding rocks. The rocks wreaked havoc on my face as I had little protection after the initial blow. I have no recollection of the actual event.

I only know any of that because I saw the x-rays and asked a lot of questions. I just remember waking up to a massive headache and a lot of people looking at me like I was the elephant man. Apparently, there had been some minor reconstruction. Many of my teeth were, unfortunately, in the way of whatever power tools were needed to make that happen, so they were considered collateral damage and removed.

It took quite a bit of surgical expertise to bring me back to my original "baby face," but to my eventual relief, it was mostly successful. The remainder of the dental surgery took years but eventually failed to bring back my slightly gap-toothed, devilish smile so admired by my mother and my childhood sweetheart. (I might add here that an eye orbit is a very delicate structure. Once it's crushed and put back together with a heavy gauge chicken wire, it will allow you to pick up radio stations in Des Moines, Iowa, from Bangor, Maine.)

The next "accident" was a few years later. It had a name but probably not one I could pronounce in Samoan, so we'll just call him

Bear because everyone else did. Apparently, Bear had a girlfriend (in his mind.) She was a waitress at the local NCO club, and I was having a casual conversation with her from my seat close to the bar. Bear informed me of his telepathic relationship with her via open-ended threat, to which I gave my usual, well-thought-out response.

I explained to Bear that if his name wasn't Clint and he didn't smell like cigar smoke and a trail-dusted poncho, I would continue my conversation with his imaginary girlfriend. That's when he made the fatal error of pulling his shirt over his head in order to remove it. I assumed this was to prepare himself for a traditional "haka" or some other Samoan tradition.

To me, that was a clear act of war, but anyone who had ever seen a Gunsmoke barfight knew what to do. While his shirt covered his head, I punched him in the area of his face as hard as I possibly could. He didn't budge an inch. As I look back on it, I am certain that he didn't even realize I had punched him. Clearly, he had consumed far more medicine than I had and was unaware of the retaliatory habits of Festus Haggen or any other frequenter of Western saloons.

Luckily, I dodged the ham that came at me but caught the bottle partially in the jaw. It was a glancing blow but caused me to expedite my exit from that particular drinking establishment. A friend hustled me out, and his friend(s) stopped his advance. The rest is NCO club lore. Some days later, even I was told of my storied courage under duress. Fear and pain are often motivators that appear to be acts of courage.

Just to make anyone interested in anatomy aware, the jaw-bone is connected to the eye orbit via hinged skull bone, so it is recommended that one not venture into the path of oncoming vehicles after having that particular surgery.

Alcohol, even if medicinal (ahem), cannot prevent the high-pitched, little girl scream that is produced if that alignment is disturbed. I am certain that local dogs were aware of my pain but probably assumed it was too late to come to my aid. It was inaudible to humans and surely suppressed by some weird mixture of testosterone and the medicine.

So, having had two encounters with near catastrophic results, I made the decision to lessen my medicinal intake and keep my mouth shut as much as I could manage.

I went about the business of tooth extraction via dentist rather than Samoan pummeling. It was a long and arduous process but much needed as the expense and inconvenience of having a continuously altering oral device was hugely expensive.

The teeth took some getting used to, but now I'm comfortable with them. Stitches in your lips on more than one occasion will do that. At first, they are very sharp, so it is important to know where they are in proximity to the meat when indulging in carnivorous activities. Failure to pay attention will result in unbearable pain if, in fact, one chews the inside of their own mouth. Again, alcohol, even if used for medicinal purposes (ahem), will not reduce the consequences of that sudden lapse in judgment.

Sometimes plastic teeth have their own internal guidance system. They can slip off a pork chop bone or slide on a piece of gristle and literally chew your face off in a matter of seconds. They are mean-spirited and made from demon horns and other debris from the nether regions.

I have a set of very expensive porcelain dentures that I can only bring out when I'm seated above carpeted floors. We have porcelain tile in our home, so I have to be careful not to drop them. If I do, they will break into a thousand zillion shards that could possibly put out the dog's eye or worse, cause a toe to be impaled in the middle of the night. They will cut through even the thinnest lettuce and pulverize meat to the point that digestion is benefitted, as is my overall constitution.

The problem with the new porthelain teeth ith that they are a bit thicker and require thome getting yuthed to. They, altho, are a lot tharper and make quick, tiny cutth on my lipth if I eat too fatht.

I really love bacon. Everyone who knowth me knowth that.

Y'all take care and laugh when your mouth alloweth it!

Proverbs 17:22

A merry heart doeth good like a medicine: but a broken spirit drieth the bones.

BANNER DAY!

FAILURE TO READ THIS WILL RESULT IN CONTINUED AGING AND SEVERE WEIGHT GAIN AND GNARLY LITTLE BUMPS ON YOUR FACE THAT OOZE AND SOME OTHER STUFF!

THE WARNING BANNERS for the newest derivative of the pandemic continue to make their way into every facet of media. They have become an automatic attachment anytime the word is mentioned. They've become a bit of a cliché, almost a punishment for daring to speak of it without permission from the giant heads who claim to have all the facts.

Every time I see them, I think of purchasing my first labeled pack of Marlboros. I saw the white banner on the side that said something about "The surgeon General warns that smoking may" whatever. I trusted their sage advice. I assumed that a surgeon who had achieved the rank of general was a fairly knowledgeable medical spokesman.

So, I decided that I no longer wanted to drive or rope cattle like the Marlboro man if it entailed coughing up a lung. That's when I did the obviously prudent thing and switched to Winston Lights . . . for my health. It wasn't that they wouldn't kill me; it was that they would cause me to live longer with a full set of lungs. After all, they were "lights." Thereafter, I watched NASCAR rather than Gunsmoke, which helped me acclimate.

Then, there was the Michelob Light of my youth. It, too, was better for me somehow. I had enjoyed many a Michelob until such time as the Light became the better gimmick. I was convinced that less of something was being filtered through my kidneys, and I would certainly never have to suffer any liver disease or other slow and painful deaths. It was much better to wrap my car around a light pole than suffer through a slow and painful end. Besides, it strengthened my spine and assisted me in my shyness; something everyone who knows me will understand. Stop laughing. This is serious.

Being older and much wiser, I've done the same thing with coffee. I mix my Dunkin' Donuts Medium Roast with decaf because it helps me control my blood pressure somehow, and I will live longer without clogged arteries or some other such medical wizardry.

Never mind that I drink three cups (at least) in the morning and use two artificial sugars in each cup. That's six a day. I'm assuming that these cleanses my arteries like Soft Bubbles in the toilet, until some medical professional tells me otherwise.

Then there's the sweet tea also made with sugar substitute (derived from sugar, of course) packets. I live in Florida, so sweet tea is a staple and high in caffeine, so it makes perfect sense that something dilutes other somethings in order to produce lower cholesterol and a more acceptable blood pressure reading. I don't need to know why; I just need to heed the warning.

For math's sake, let's just assume that I drink at least eight packets a day. That's at least 240 packets a month no matter how you compute it. You really don't need an abacus or microprocessor to figure out that I'm dumping what could later be discovered as carcinogenic nuclear waste into my system at a rate higher than the law of class action lawsuits will allow.

Then there's the stuff I put under my arms, the stuff that holds my teeth in, the stuff that keeps my hair in place, the foot odor spray for my tennis shoes, and the bathroom spray that serves as an anti-septic cleaner, even though the label says it won't.

Danger is everywhere. I pity the ladies of the sixties who used enough Aqua Net to slow a wind turbine, but at least the ozone survived even though it was severely damaged. I'm sure that is the reason for global warming, though. We weren't warned that this was even a remote possibility until it was too late. Who knew "Eve of Destruction" was a song about women's hairspray? Not to point fingers, but Brylcreem did warn that it only took a dab to keep a man's hair in place. So, there were obvious warnings.

Lest we forget, I live in Florida, and bugs die much faster when sprayed with chemicals. I invite the young, highly educated pest control chemist into my home once a month. He mixes stuff for ants, then a powder for spiders, and, of course, the barrier for pal-metto bugs and the yearly inspection for termites. I am certain, because they tell me so, that these chemical agents will not kill my pets, even if my pets are possums and squirrels. I'm not sure how that is accomplished, but I'm sure there is a giant head some-where who concocts these potions in such a way that my animal friends and I are fully protected from potential harm. I trust them as I would my own mother who told me that "Soap Sally" would come in the night and turn me into soap if I didn't take a bath.

I know all of this because there have been warning labels and ban-ners all of my life. I still have the labels on my mattresses because I know that the mattress inspectors will enter my home someday and issue me a fine for removing them.

All that to say this: I've been vaccinated for every disease known to man, it seems. They were required for enrollment in schools when I was younger. They were also required in order to enlist in the armed forces. I have never had a fatal disease. Not yet. But when that time comes, if it comes, I am certain that it will be the result of the Lord's will and not that I didn't heed a banner warning. It won't be because I didn't read the warning or because I believed that the warning wasn't important. It will be because I am a sinner, and the result of that sin is death.

Hence the proof that we are all sinners and that there is hope beyond the warning banner.

When we all get to heaven, because everyone believes they are going to heaven, I wonder if the ones who are turned away will complain because there weren't enough warnings about their condition?

If you've never taken the time to read the warnings, it may be time to pick up a Bible and read the truth about eternity. There are warning labels and banners that give you a pretty clear picture of what happens if you don't heed the warnings.

Maybe we should require a warning label on the front of all Bibles. It may be coming to that, anyway.

Between Joey and Jesus

WELL, WE WORKED hard all of our lives and finally were able to move to the lake. We're both getting better from our respective disasters, Lynn from her fall and leg injuries and me from my torn cartilage and ultimate hip replacement. It was touch and go there for a while, especially since neither of us could really lift anything and were about to make the biggest move either of us had ever made. We needed help, and neither of us were very good at asking. We've always done for ourselves, mostly, but we saw we needed help, so we prayed and prayed again.

Then came the troops. First there was Janene (mom) and Jamie (beautiful daughter), folks from our church who we absolutely adore. They came in on two different days to help us pack. This, after we had asked them to come over and help clean when we were showing the house, truly servants' hearts. We could never thank them enough.

Enter Leigh and Mike (niece and nephew), virtual working tornadoes. We had a lot of stuff in the yard and patio that had to go: an old boat trailer, grill, patio furniture . . . stuff! They brought their friend, "Guy," who was about to haul it all off in his trailer when the junk man Pedro arrived. He was more than happy to assist. In the end, Pedro had a good day. Guy hauled off a great desk, and Leigh and Mike became our favorite niece and nephew, forever! (Sorry to the rest of you, but they earned it!)

Then it became clear that we were falling behind. Neither of us were able to really bend over a lot, so finishing packing became virtually impossible. Lynn trudged ahead, but I still had to be very careful of swelling due to a recent bout with bursitis. If you've ever been there, you know what that means. It was a bad place to be in light of our situation.

We needed another trailer besides the one I had already packed. So, I called the U-Haul folks and set out to pick up the trailer. As I got into my truck, I literally prayed this prayer. "Lord, we need more help. Could you send us someone who can help us out?" It was literally a "Jesus, take the wheel" moment.

As I got to the end of my street. There was a truck broken down at the stop sign. I impatiently went around him. Out of the corner of my eye, I saw someone I thought I recognized. I couldn't place him, and I went ahead. I was on a tight schedule. I wasn't out of the neighborhood when "something" told me to go back and see if I could help that guy out. So, I begrudgingly turned around, knowing it would set me back, and there he came, rounding the corner. Apparently, his truck was okay. I flagged him down!

As it turned out, I did know him. His name was Joey. Years ago (at least ten), I had gone to his house and prayed with him about some personal demons he was fighting. He remembered me, and I told him about my predicament. He said he'd be over the next day. Sure enough, he was, and he brought a friend. I can't begin to tell you what a tremendous help they were. They packed the remainder of the boxes and completely loaded the second trailer. Then they vacuumed and mopped the entire house. They set a bunch of throwaway things out on the street, quite a large pile, and agreed to come and get it all the next morning and take it all to the dump, altogether about twelve hours of work. Done! Finished! Out of the house!

We had already arranged for help at the lake. The pod would be here Friday, and the help here was in abundance. Good friends and neighbors were all around, so we'd be fine.

I said all of that to say all of this. Prayer is a wonderful thing. God knows what you need and when you need it, but you have to trust Him. The Bible says this:

"And we know that all things work together for good to them that love God, to them who are the called according to his purpose" (Rom. 8:28). Surely God has a plan and purpose for us here at the lake, and he has provided all we need to serve.

Joey called me a couple of days ago and said this: "Stan, I honestly believe that God caused my truck to break down so that you and I could connect. It's been running perfectly ever since." Knowing what I now know, I believe that to be exactly what happened I believe this as well: God used all of these people in a way that only He could to put us exactly where He wanted us. We so appreciate the hands and feet (and backs) that God sent us in our time of need. Thank you all, and thank you, Jesus!

Psalm 46:1–3

God is our refuge and strength, an ever-present help in trouble. Therefore, we will not fear, though the earth gives way and the mountains fall into the heart of the sea, though its waters roar and foam and the mountains quake with their surging.

Apatheism

YOU HEARD ABOUT God as a child. You didn't really accept the idea that there was something or someone greater than you. You listened, but you didn't necessarily care. There was no epiphany during Sunday school and certainly nothing in the service that would make you believe such an absurdity. Your parents required you to go, so you tried to make the best of it.

You didn't understand what the fuss was all about. This Jesus dying and all of that. How could anyone know why He died? And that resurrection thing? No way! You didn't understand the concept that people would gather and sing together from a song book, much less listen to stories from another book, one they deemed "holy," whatever that means.

You scoffed at the idea that anything or anyone was really thinking this through. It was clear that they were all just catering to each other and not really attached to their own God. If He existed at all, He certainly wasn't involved with each of them personally. You smiled and shook hands a lot. You acted as if you were one of them, but it was just to keep the peace. Soon, you'd be on your own, and you laughed at the idea that you would need any God to help you out.

When teachers and friends asked about your religious views, you simply shrugged and said whatever they wanted to hear. That was the only response that made any sense. Otherwise, they'd try to convince you, and you'd had enough of that. You never really accepted all the hype. People were still hateful in general, and everyone eventually died. Why wouldn't God fix that?

It didn't matter when the preacher talked about a holy, righteous, or even a good God. You didn't really grasp the concept. Those were just words, adjectives to describe the indescribable. You mentally scoffed at the idea that God would speak to anyone personally. At least, you'd never heard Him.

You remembered that time when those guys went off to war and the entire church gathered to pray for them. You wondered then what they must be thinking. You wondered why they put their lives on the line, and you secretly hoped you wouldn't have to go. When you found out you wouldn't be required to serve, you were thankful but not toward any particular entity, just relieved, mostly.

You rejected the whole idea of war and freedom and dying for any cause. You went to the funerals of the two guys who didn't return. "It was just their time to go," you'd say. You watched their grieving mom as she took the flag and thought, "Where's your God now?"

When that neighbor's little girl died suddenly and you went with your mom to take them food and pay your respects, you realized that no good God would allow such a thing. You'd heard just about enough of "God's will" and "God's goodness." It didn't make any sense that God would "take her home" so early in her life. You couldn't imagine that a good God would do such a thing.

You figured it all out and headed for college. There, you met like-minded people who genuinely laughed at the idea that God even existed, much less that He was personally involved in every aspect of their lives. You became disturbed as you studied all the reasons the planet was dying from climate change and wondered how people could be so ignorant to not see that their "God" had vacated the premises. There were a few "Christian" kids there, but you quickly shooed them off. No way did you want to get involved in that whole "church mess" again.

You graduated with honors and began your adult life with a good job. You'd learned how to be self-sufficient and understood the ways of the world. You bristled at the thought that of anyone or anything keeping you from a successful life. You were a well-educated, self-motivated powerhouse of information gleaned from the best minds. You were a self-made man.

Then you met a woman who literally blew your socks off. She was bright and beautiful. You talked about everything. You were a perfect fit. It was perfect until she asked you about your religious views. You explained that you had no real connection with any religion but that you were raised in church. You had no real religious motivations. You visibly shrugged as you talked. She looked disappointed, but you were sure you could play the Christian part if you had to. Still, you made it seem like you were genuinely interested.

When the call came that she had been in an accident, you realized it wasn't really love when you saw that she would need lifelong care. You were sad for her, but you went about the business of distancing yourself. That was easier than you thought. You were almost ashamed when she passed away, just not enough to attend the funeral. Church again. Once again, you rejected the idea that God was good or close or righteous. It just didn't add up.

You concentrated on your career. You moved up, met the right people, and attended the right events. You searched for someone to share life with. You met the girl of your dreams. You married and started a family. You had a little girl together. She was the apple of your eye. You wanted to show her your world and help her along. She was so inquisitive. She asked about God. You told her you didn't actually believe in God. It felt strange to say that, but you didn't want to lie. She stared at the ground for a minute as if to say, "Okay then, I won't either." Life was great! You loved watching her grow.

After a lifetime of successes, you became ill, very ill. The doctors agreed on a treatment plan. You focused all of your energy on getting better. After a punishing few months of treatment, the doctor looked you in the eye and told you the cancer had spread. You just knew there were options. You asked a million questions, but in the end, the doctor mostly just stared and said that they had done all they could do.

You didn't know where to turn. There was no way you were going to leave your wife and child alone in the world, helpless. You thought back over the years and the many times you had ignored God, but for some reason, you reached for the Bible your dad had brought you when you were really low. You began to read like a child with their first book. You somehow remembered a lot of the words. This time, you felt them. You couldn't imagine that He would hear you after all these years of rejecting Him, but you screamed it aloud anyway.

"WHERE ARE YOU NOW, GOD?"

"Right here . . . where I've always been," said a still, small voice.

Psalm 23

*The L*ORD *is my shepherd; I shall not want.*
He maketh me to lie down in green pastures:
he leadeth me beside the still waters.
He restoreth my soul: he leadeth me in the paths
of righteousness for his name's sake.
Yea, though I walk through the valley of the shadow
of death, I will fear no evil: for thou art with
me; thy rod and thy staff they comfort me.
Thou preparest a table before me in the presence of my enemies:
thou anointest my head with oil; my cup runneth over.
Surely goodness and mercy shall follow me all the days of
*my life: and I will dwell in the house of the L*ORD *forever.*

The Oughtamen Empire

IT AMAZES ME the number of self-appointed experts there are in the world. In virtually every discussion, their counsel always comes from some self-generated wealth of insight. Somehow, they have developed a more keen and enlightened view of any and all scenarios surrounding any subject.

It is as if they have received some personal revelation from Almighty God that allows them to speak on his behalf as if they possess some supernaturally granted wisdom. Sometimes this wisdom is gained overnight or immediately in moments of crises.

Nowhere is this more prevalent than in the media. More often than not, there are panels of various experts appointed by some unseeable, non-vetted higher power to give the appearance of a holier than thou, pre-ordained magistrate with only one objective: to tell us what we "oughta" think and what we "oughta" do.

We have medical doctors, psychologists, politicians, and a plethora of ordained and omniscient newscasters offering their highly educated opinions on virtually any and all subjects. I find it amazing that these folks are so immediately available and so important to the cause of perfecting humankind.

Depending on which station you watch, the "much more informed" and highly influential "oughta-men" take up space that could otherwise be spent discerning what is and isn't applicable to your situation. That is the freedom you have in America. Everyone doesn't need to agree on every matter.

The effort to convince and conform others to their completely thought-out opinion has become the focus of media. However, an opinion that is duplicated and distributed across a wide spectrum isn't opinion at all. It is an attempt to persuade, either by implication or repetition, who will be placed in the seats of power. That is the chief end of media.

Those with an implied, heightened sense of morality are the appointed guides that take us to the great throne of moral direction. The degree to which we comply is computed via poll numbers indicating what percentage of voters will comply. This is the calculation that decides our direction because we are morally obligated to follow the Great Unseen Oughtaman who holds the map to our ultimate destination.

Indeed, these are the Keepers of the Moral Compass. The points on the compass are vague but generally depicted as fairness, equality, and justice with the path to magnetic North being political affiliation. The degree to which we comply is the degree to which we will bow to their teaching.'

Here's the problem with the Oughtamen. They possess only imagined wisdom. Their compass points are unachievable goals. Mankind will never become just or equal or fair or even politically purposed because we are inherently opposed to those virtues.

In social media, we are now in the process of conforming to some new, omniscient form of these wise men. Fact-checkers are the resident Oughta-men, with powers that exceed simple warnings. They can decide truth and tell us what we oughta say or oughta not say in virtually any discussion. All they need to do is look at their compass and decide how far off the point we are and how we can best be punished for wandering off the path of their own considered opinion. That is the unforgivable sin.

Their version of fairness is determined by algorithm, not wisdom. The number of times one misses the mark within a certain period of time determines the length of the predetermined, algorithmic punishment. Some can even be sent to social media hell, permanently banned from social media for the most egregious sins, non-compliance being the deadliest of those sins.

Failure to agree with "new norms" will get you a cyber cell. Any comment or response denouncing the new king or opposition to any perversion or (gasp) defending the innocent or opposing religious views are all damnable sins.

How absolutely omnipotent they have become. All hail the Omniscient Oughtamen!

All that to say this: Wisdom comes from God. It's determined by His actual omniscience. Study His Word and ask Him for wisdom before accepting the words of self-ordained Oughtamen.

The wise will rarely point to themselves as the arbiters of truth or justice. Only the foolish would think they have that kind of power.

James 3:17

But the wisdom that comes from heaven is first of all pure; then peace-loving, considerate, submissive, full of mercy and good fruit, impartial and sincere.

Worldview

I FIND MYSELF BEING drawn into daily politics no matter how I try to avoid them. For some reason, it matters to me what's going on in the world even though I'm convinced that it will go the way it is supposed to because that is the proverbial "way of the world."

The subtle things, the lean toward acceptable transgression, the non-ordained messages allegedly from God and the futility with which we all endeavor to explain ourselves become an exercise in pride and most certainly a visible compass by which we can measure the "progress" of the world in general.

In Christianity, now being heaped onto the pile of religious zealotry, it is called "the world" because it lacks order and goodness and will invariably seek the path that moves away from God and into chaos. The world has a leader. I've met him.

The world is diametrically opposed to the things of God. So, a more tolerant morality, where inclusiveness and equality are the supreme gauges of our goodness, falls short of any godly direction. "Lord, have mercy" is the only plea I can make in a world so entrenched in chaos that it seeks the wrong cure for diseases of the heart.

I tend to take a back seat and watch the world nosedive into self-destruction. I'm certain that there aren't a lot of places I can be of use except to write about the things I see and encourage others to run toward the things of God and away from the immorality that so easily entangles us all.

I accept that all things are the providence of God, and for me to step into the ring and challenge all the running bulls is not always the prudent thing to do. Wisdom comes from God. Choosing our battles is both wise and necessary. Winning them on this side of heaven requires intercession from God Himself. "His will be done" is a necessary determination when offering opinions.

I am guilty of transgressions like any other. I believe the difference is that I find it necessary to make the effort to see things from a godly perspective. I'm not sure that I always do, but that is the effort. Surely it's not my function to condemn. That's a fairly easy task. There are a lot of things wrong in the world. If I point them out, know that it isn't my condemnation that matters. Only God has the power and authority to convict. Perhaps your conversation should be with Him. Allow me to introduce you.

I see my own sin and find that I can hardly be the one to point to the world and pronounce them guilty of their transgressions, even though I am saved from ultimate punishment for those sins because of what Jesus did on the cross. That is the view I take. It doesn't come from any political persuasion or societal influence. I read and study the book and listen to those whom I believe are well versed and called for the purpose of teaching the truth of the Word of God.

My effort is to point folks to that higher view, the one that points to the one, true Savior of the world and the one who will ultimately have His way on it, in it, and above it. Without His direction, we are subject to the values the world sees as good and acceptable.

I don't expect everyone to view the world as I do, nor do I intend to exceed the boundaries of my own calling. I do, however, expect that I will be allowed my perspective and will continue to stand for those things that don't appeal to the world's interpretation of what is right or wrong.

I am, by virtue of my own salvation, required to be separate from the world. I do not think, nor do I aspire to be or act like those who choose the world as their source of morality. I generally do not appeal to those who object to what the Bible says.

It is therefore necessary that I sometimes personally cut to the chase and appeal to those who seek to "make the world a better place" by attempting to remove my point of view so that theirs can be more widely accepted. That effort is the mark of a failed and unsourced vision.

Your title, be it fact-checker, influencer, critic, or even teacher, does not, nor will it ever, demand my compliance to the prevailing morality because you are none of those things in my world, nor are you a source of wisdom in His.

The sensitivity with which we are all required to speak is not something that demands my full attention. I believe decorum and discretion are certainly reliable objectives but not at the expense of truth.

Titus 2:11–12

For the grace of God has appeared that offers salvation to all people. It teaches us to say "No" to ungodliness and worldly passions, and to live self-controlled, upright and godly lives in this present age.

Choosing Battles

I AM A CHRISTIAN and a proud Southern boy. Unapologetic on both counts, both by the grace of God. If that offends you. Read no further.

The cross is a symbol of the death of Jesus Christ. An empty cross is a reminder that he is no longer on that cross but that He is risen.

I personally identify with that cross because I know what happened there. I know that a terrible but necessary "injustice" occurred on that cross. Men condemned the Son of God to die without regard for the good that He had done or the message he came to give. I also know that He willingly gave His life so that I might live. He could have halted the entire event, but He chose to die for me as payment for my sin because it was required of Him for sinful men to reconcile with Holy God!

When I see the cross, I remember the sacrifice Jesus made for me. When a Muslim sees the cross, he doesn't see what I see. He sees a prophet and the infidels who follow him. When a Jewish person sees the cross, he is not convinced that this man Jesus was, and is, the Messiah, the Savior of the world. The same is true of anyone who believes differently about the identity of Jesus.

The cross is a symbol. For those who have come to know Jesus, it is a symbol of the hope that lies in Him, the hope of eternal life. It is how we view it that is important. It is not a structure to worship. That would make it an idol. It is an object that Christians every-where identify as the promise of eternal life given by the one who died there. Removing it wouldn't change my view or the events that took place on it any more than it would change my eternal destination.

Likewise, a rainbow is a sign from God that promises the world will never be destroyed by another flood. I accept that promise as I do to all the promises of God. When I see an actual rainbow, I remember the promise of God. That's why He creates them, as a testimony of his love for his creation and a reminder of His promise.

For that reason, a rainbow flag is somewhat offensive to me as it is used in a way that attempts to mock the very promise of God. As a Christian, I look at that flag differently because of what it represents to me. I also realize that the world is going to be the world, and my being offended won't change anything. I also know that God will not be mocked and that judgment is His alone. I have no intention of removing anyone's flag.

Symbols, like beauty, are in the eye of the beholder. It may be a symbol, but what it represents is left to the interpretation of the one viewing it. It's that simple, really. When I see the Dixie flag, I am reminded of a proud history, a heritage steeped in gentlemanly behavior and Southern charm, wonderful, welcoming people, hospitable and gracious, and fierce when they are confronted with demands that counter their individuality. I am also reminded of a time when men stood against tyranny and fought to their last breath, not for slavery but against tyranny because duty and honor demanded it. Others have a different perspective. I get that!

Removing a flag or statue or painting won't change my heritage. It won't change my heart. It won't change my mind because whether you view it as a symbol of hate or a symbol of tradition, it is still just a symbol. It can't change a heart. Nor can it change history.

In the grand scheme of things, a flag doesn't mean very much to those who view it in a bad light, but it means a lot to those who view it in terms of their own heritage. Therein lies the rub.

Perhaps if we take our focus off the flags and concern ourselves with our eternal citizenship, we'll see the world from heaven's perspective, the only one that matters. No one can take from you what is imbedded in your heart. Even the ones who die for their country leave their flags behind.

These "hot button" issues are designed to steal our joy. They are earthly matters. We shouldn't let them overwhelm us. We should think about eternal things. Think about heaven. Think about how we can take someone with us.

Due to my very Southern heritage, it is difficult for me not to participate in the fray, but I have higher duties to assume. I simply must set my sights on the kingdom of heaven. That is where I will plant my eternal flag and the only place I would rather be than Dixieland!

Matthew 6:33

But seek you first the kingdom of God, and his righteousness; and all these things shall be added unto you.

Comedy Stored

THE WORLD HAS lost its sense of humor. I guess it was time. Sad to see it go, but I'm going to continue the struggle because in the immortal words of Martin Luther, "Here I stand. I can do no other." (How dare me.)

I stand on the side of joy, not necessarily happiness, looking down on a world drowning (metaphorically) in her own misery. It doesn't seem fair that I should be in a position to watch it all disappear. Still, worthy or not, God has given me eyes that see. I've learned to trust them and Him.

I choose to see humor where I probably shouldn't. Chaos isn't really funny. It is a product manufactured in a place most have decided to ignore. The idea of living in a divine comedy actually becomes a possibility, though that theology is disturbing. I only use the concept to express my view of the world, which is primarily, "Laugh, and the world laughs with you."

I am aware of the wars that rage but try desperately not to engage with the foolishness that surrounds virtually every opposing idea or dissenting opinion. Moral judgment is above my paygrade but pointing out God's judgment is well within the confines of my personal calling, as much as it is with any professing Christian.

Sometimes I take it to the edge and laugh at things I shouldn't. Sometimes I see the futility in the world and choose to divest myself of any of its foolishness by pointing out that very foolishness. That's what I do. I really, really don't choose to engage the terminally offended at any level. If I'm your enemy, you've given me more power than I deserve or want.

I see the folly in the vague, unwritten rules of morality as if there are ways to escape the established boundaries. It appears as though folks have become subject to some ever-evolving level of scrutiny by an indeterminate moral authority that many recognize as omniscient but are not quite able to identify as God. Maybe it's not humor I find in that. Maybe it is that I see the need to point away from the folly and toward what I know to be the truth.

I stand on the side of the ancient rules that are already written, literally in stone, literally by the hand of God. I don't find it amusing or in the least entertaining to witness the depths and distances folks will go to follow socially adapted rules to the contrary. I do not find the inevitability of eternal separation from God amusing, in any way.

I stand on the gospel of Jesus Christ and the truth of His death, burial, and resurrection. I see and understand the seriousness of promoting that truth above all else. If that is offensive to you, my best advice is to at least form a decent battle plan before aiming at me personally because when you do that, I find it hilarious. You, in fact, arm me because it affirms that you lack any real understanding of the war.

I guess a sense of humor is just the shield God gave me. Know that I have a sword as well. Also know that it won't be a fair fight.

I intend to live in peace wherever possible (see below) but have the certainty of an ever-present, ever demanding war. My job is to contend for the faith. I'm going to do that in as lighthearted a manner as I can possibly achieve without giving into the ridiculous efforts of an already defeated enemy.

How do you like me now?

Romans 12:18

If it is possible, as far as it depends on you,
live at peace with everyone.

Ransackin'

As soon as we heard the news, we grabbed our back packs and headed down to the dollar store in Crescent City (Florida). What we'd heard was that you could just go in and take whatever you wanted as long as it didn't amount to a thousand bucks. Most people here had never even seen a thousand bucks, so they went just to pick up a few things.

Apparently, we weren't the first to find out. There was a near traffic jam all the way back from the Winn-Dixie just like when Darnell Roberson would drive his old Ford truck into town. It took forever, but we could see the parkin' lot was full, so we waited our turn. We figgered there'd probly be at least a few boxes of Pop Tarts left back in the storeroom and maybe some more Slim Jims we could use for bait.

By the time we got there, Sheriff Hardcastle had pulled in, lights a flashin' and was already wailin' on Dr. Jenkins' son, Davey. Apparently, young Davey had hooked a chain up to the charcoal rack out front and tried to yank it off the wall with his F150. That made Sheriff Hardcastle madder than a baptized cat, and he just started slappin' him around and yellin' like a ruptured goose. I'm sure that Davey was unaware that the good sheriff had taken a fancy to the widow Pierce (who owns the store) and that he had been slowly introducin' hisself after his wife died last February. That was probly the first real whoopin' that boy had ever got.

There was people runnin' in an out carryin' stuff in feed bags and laundry baskets and whatever else they could find. It was near pandemonium except for everybody was takin' turns holdin' the door open for the older folks. They were all confused and tried to pay anybody who would listen, but folks just kept yellin' that everything was free and for them to go on. Ol' man Pickens yelled out for people to stop and think about what they was doin', but apparently, folks had already thought it through. Free was free, and if they could do it in California, we could too.

Cheryl Ann Pierce took a yellow plastic Adirondack chair from the stack and sat by the door watchin' folks she'd known all her life runnin' in and out, stealin' from her kids. She was barely makin' it as it was, but she knew the Lord would see her through. He always did. She took another drag off her fake cigarette and shook her head as people filed through. She wasn't wearin' that fake smile she put on most every mornin', though. She'd owned the store for nearly eighteen years and couldn't believe what she was seein'. Nobody said good morning, and they sure wouldn't look her in the eye.

Ol' Cletus Montrose even got in on the action. He just about cleaned out the paper goods. We knew he'd take it all down to the huntin' camp, and nobody would know the differnce. He hauled off enough paper plates and plasticware to last the season. *No sense overdoin it*, he thought.

By the end of the day, Cheryl was handin' stuff out rather than have folks trackin' in all the charcoal dust from the mess the Jenkins boy had made. All that was left was mostly soap stuff and beauty products. There weren't a large callin' for that stuff, but some of the older ladies used it for church, so she kept a supply of it.

The place was almost empty by the time she was done for the day. There was no way to resupply it, so she guessed she'd be shuttin' it down soon. She'd find somethin' else to do. She'd developed a lot of skills since owning the store, and everybody knew her. She'd be fine.

The next day at Sunday mornin' service, the preacher spoke the most powerful sermon we'd ever heard about robbin' and stealin'. It was like he was mad at everybody! He wuz spittin' and hollerin' like nobody had ever heard. He musta slammed his Bible on the pulpit twenty times, and there weren't a lot of amenin' goin' on neither. It was dead silent. Even the hymns were flat. It wuz like everybody was feelin' guilty all at once.

His closing prayer was for the town and the people in it. He prayed that the devil would be cast out and that folks would realize the error of their ways. It was a tough thing to listen to, fer sure, but nobody said nothin', but you could tell everybody wuz uncomfortable. That much was certain; lotsa squirmin' in the seats and throat clearin'.

After the scoldin', Cheryl was the first to go down and pray. She usually was since her husband Glen had died. He was kinda like the town hero. Everyone remembered when he'd saved those kids from that church van that blew up on Highway 17 after it had gone off into the gulley. He got 'em all out before the fire got outta control, but he paid the price for a few weeks before he finally passed on. The whole town showed up for his funeral.

That afternoon, there was another almost traffic jam in town. The cars were lined up at the dollar store again. We couldn't imagine why because it was mostly empty, but there were people runnin' in and out just like before. We wondered what was left that everybody missed.

We pulled in and saw Cheryl's blue Camry parked in front as usual. When we came through the door, and there was Cheryl, directin' folks as to what went where while the pastor and three of the deacons from the Baptist church was stockin' shelves as fast as they could get the goods out of the feed bags and laundry baskets stacked outside the door. Some of the bags were empty but had money inside.

There was a run at the Winn-Dixie on soap products and paper goods. We saw ol' Cletus with a full truck of that stuff headed back to the dollar store. Gerald Miller and his son were paintin' and puttin' in light bulbs. His wife, Celia, was cleanin' everthing she could touch, the same way she did the church. There were new brackets on the charcoal rack, and all the windows had been cleaned. The Jenkins boy had pressure washed just about the whole dang place, and the good doctor had sent a crew out to clean up the landscape and fix the sign that was startin' to flicker. The place looked brand spankin' new.

Bart and Clint from B&C Barbecue had already pulled their smoker in and was givin' away chicken and ribs as fast as they could pull 'em off the fire. People was puttin' money in the donation bucket so fast that Bart had to put out a trashcan he'd bought from Cheryl. It was something he did every year, but this time it was differnt. The money was going to Cheryl and her kids for the money and time she'd lost as a result of the day of lootin' and ransackin'. It was a wonder to behold.

The next week, we saw the church offerin' was nearly ten times what it had been. The pastor said we'd be feedin' a lot of people at the Christmas dinner this year. We always did, but this time it'd be differnt.

I guess we ain't cut like them folks in California. We all know what we did was wrong. Stealin' is stealin'! That's all there is to it. It ain't like we don't know the differnce between right and wrong. We just got caught up in the moment, I guess. That happens when you wake the devil. Ain't nothing free, and there's a lot worse things than bein' poor, like stealin' just to be stealin'.

I'm thinkin' God has forgiven us for our temporary meanness. He's good like that, but it all goes to show that people can turn into animals anytime. All it takes is one bad apple, just like in the beginning.

2 Peter 3:9

The Lord is not slow in keeping his promise, as some understand slowness. Instead, he is patient with you, not wanting anyone to perish, but everyone to come to repentance.

***This story was gleaned from a hilarious conversation with our friend, Mike Easley, on 12/1/21.*

The Coffee Maker

THIS MORNING, I couldn't make coffee. I panicked and started looking for reasons for the sudden loss of power to the coffee maker. After a few moments, I noticed that the plug had become unseated. There ain't no coffee when there ain't no power goin' to the coffee maker. That's science right there!

I trust my coffee maker to make good coffee. I believe it heats the water and distributes it over the ground beans, creating my morning brew. I believe the beans grow well in certain climates and that the water comes from the lake via my well. The filters and cups and cream all work together to produce what I refer to as my morning coffee. It's a process.

Science is involved in each aspect of that. I believe all of those sciences, from the unseen electrons that move faster to heat the coffee to the water filtration system that causes the water to be free from various impurities. I can't see the electrons or the impurities or even the beans once they are ground, but I know beyond any doubt that they exist. I have learned to trust all the elements involved in making my coffee. I trust science not because I am a scientist or even because a percentage of scientists agree. Rather, I believe that my coffee maker will produce coffee consistently because it has proven to be capable of that function.

I believe all of that because each morning, the evidence is set before me in the form of a perfectly brewed cup of coffee. I add other products to this already perfect science project in the form of pasteurized milk and refined sugar in one form or another. I stir and sip and voila, my coffee exists. It's science, but it tastes like a miracle in my mouth. I love my coffee!

I don't get eggs or bacon from my coffee maker because I know that those require different methods of preparation and cooking. I can depend on my coffee maker to do only so much. It produces coffee at the level I expect. I can't rely on it for bacon because it isn't designed for that purpose. I have faith that it will produce coffee as needed. No amount of wishing or hoping will make my coffee maker a bacon machine.

I believe my coffee maker exists to make coffee. I believe it makes good coffee. I believe that is the reason for its existence. I believe that the science involved in producing my coffee bears witness to the accuracy of the science involved. I have no doubts about the science. I can taste the coffee.

I also believe in God. I can't see God, but I have no doubt that He exists. I have read and studied the evidence as it is presented. I can also see the evidence in nature. There is reason, order, and hope in all that God has made.

I can see a sunrise. I can understand the science of it. I can follow the idea of a spinning earth and refracted light and the movement of planets around the sun, magnetic fields, the tilt and wobble of the earth on its axis, the formation of clouds, the rain, the wind, all of that. I believe in the scientific explanations of the sunrise. The knowledge of all of the science only increases my dependency on the Creator of it.

What I can't fully understand is the beauty that accompanies these explosions. Science cannot explain, nor can anyone to complete satisfaction, how a sunrise opens the heavens and the human soul to a new day.

I can watch the seasons change, the leaves fall, and the rapid appearance of winter. I feel the cold. Then comes the spring and the summer, each moving the sun across the horizon, spawning fish, migrating birds, tadpoles turning into frogs, and larva to lizards. Tides rise and fall with the cycling moon, all put together for my viewing pleasure so that I can see and feel and be touched and even taste the salt air of a new day. There is no science that can explain the sudden outburst or the process of spiritual renewal that comes with morning.

I believe that the Bible is the inspired Word of God. Each morning I read and study it. It produces within me a better understanding of the world and a stronger belief in God. I am not just aware of the idea of God, but I am also able to converse with Him and experience His goodness. My understanding of the world is enhanced as God reveals Himself to me through His Word. I study God. My faith is increased as I pursue Him and learn to trust Him with the details of my life. I am never disappointed. I understand that He has the whole of it in His capable hands. I accept that discovery isn't creation, and that explanation is just the cold reporting of what God has produced for my (our) enjoyment.

I refer to the Bible often because studying refreshes my soul. Every day I am granted not just a scientific process but a few moments of supernatural grandeur, complimented by a symphony of birds and a reflective view of my very soul. I am always surrounded by the truth of God's Word and the knowledge that He not only created all of this but He also maintains it with a supernatural consistency.

I am reminded of His majesty and to whom all power and authority are given. I like to stay plugged in.

Each morning, I am restored to my God, my Creator, my Savior via the book provided to me by the Maker of everything, including my morning coffee. Praise God from whom all blessings flow!

Romans 1:20

For since the creation of the world God's invisible qualities— his eternal power and divine nature—have been clearly seen, being understood from what has been made, so that people are without excuse.

Romans 15:13

May the God of hope fill you with all joy and peace as you trust in him, so that you may overflow with hope by the power of the Holy Spirit.

Sins of My Other

I SERIOUSLY DOUBT IF I will ever change the opinions of those who know me in my youth. Let's just say that I wasn't tied to anything solid, so I tended to bounce from one indiscretion to the next without any sense of direction. Certainly, I was raised to be God-fearing and knew the way home; I simply chose to break with all of that and make my own way.

Some would think that foolish, and it was, in a lot of ways. I will not attempt to defend that foolishness. It was indeed a product of my youthful guidance system. I was unequipped to handle my own affairs. I stumbled and fell. As I look back, I see the many lessons I could have learned and didn't.

The problem was that my youth extended beyond its normal limits. Youthful indiscretions became habits. Habits became obsessions. Sins (transgressions) became recurring. Acknowledging them became less and less a matter of importance. I bore the chains of my own transgressions. I was indeed living the life that wasn't meant for me. Growing up just wasn't in my plan.

I was blind and deaf to the will of God. I was disobedient, considering myself liberated from the mandates of God. In a word, I ignored Him. Ignoring God has consequences. Trust me on that. Better yet, read the book of Jonah.

If not for the grace of a loving God and His love for me, I may never have achieved adulthood, if indeed that is an achievement. I might still be wandering in whatever dark corner would accept me, and I was adept at finding dark corners.

God makes people like me, people whose lives become testimonies to His goodness. Many years later, I am still adjusting to this adulthood. I often remember my indiscretions and shake my head at me and bow before the one who took me from the bondage of my own making.

Part of my life now is spent in a place of absolute gratitude for the God of my salvation, the one who saved me from myself, the one who died so that I might be forgiven.

I often reflect on my own recklessness. I am often reminded of them by folks who used to know me. "What was I thinking?" has replaced "Hold my beer" if I might use a couple of clichés to develop the thought.

I am no longer that person; though, the past does occasionally come back to haunt me. I have indeed become a new creature, but that doesn't matter to those who remember my sins. They still remember that time that I (insert foolishness here).

To those, I would simply say, better to monitor your own transgressions than to spend a lot of time concentrating on mine. I've been forgiven by the only one whose forgiveness frees me from those chains. I pray the same experience for you.

2 Corinthians 5:17

Therefore, if any man be in Christ, he is a new creature: old things are passed away; behold, all things are become new.

Shots Fired

So, I was waking up from a drug-induced sleep. Lynn walked up to me and shot me in the head with some kind of handgun, right between the eyes.

I fell back on the pillow, grabbing my head, writhing in pain. I couldn't imagine what I had said or done to cause her to just shoot me in the head without warning.

My life flashed before my eyes. At least it was quick, I thought. I tried to remember the last few days, and I couldn't even remember what we talked about before or after the surgery. My mind went blank. Of course, it did. I'd just been shot in the head!

I remember talking a lot on the way home from the hour-long drive from the hospital, but I'm not exactly sure about what. It was probably something about internal combustion engines or a laundry list of things I'd be needing for the next few days, and, of course, the obligatory driving instructions, all normal stuff in the mind of an anesthetized, slobbering passenger.

I guess I sent her off the deep end' poor thing. She'll spend the rest of her life in prison. It's kinda sad, really. I kinda hoped she'd get away with it in a strange kinda way. I knew how insensitive I could be, particularly after the anesthesia—not our first rodeo.

I kept waiting for the blood to saturate my pillow and drip to the floor. I knew it was probably an ugly scene. I hated that she had spent all that time washing all the bed clothes just to get them all bloody. There was no pain, though, and I only had myself to thank for taking her to the range all those times.

I looked up at her, trying to measure her emotional state. She was calm and cool, as usual. I'm sure she had planned it well and the cleaners were on their way. I'd miss the place, but heaven was just a shot away. I should probably thank her for the clean shot.

"Ninety-eight point four," she said. I tried to put the numbers together. I didn't know if that was a sports score or a range distance. Nothing rang a bell, so I just said, "Wath it thomething I thaid?" which is not exactly what I had planned for my last words.

She said it with a little more explanation this time. "Your temperature is nighty-eight point four."

That's when she handed me my denture case and smiled sweetly. I sat upright and put my teeth in, acting cool like nothing had happened.

"This no-touch thermometer is really cool, just like in the hospital."

I nodded and stared out the bedroom window, pondering the last few minutes before my imagined death. I really wish the anesthesia hadn't made my voice so gruff because anything I said would be taken wrong. I reflected in silence.

I would always remember how easy it was to just take me down without a hint of malice aforethought. I needed to be really grateful to her during my recovery. She really was doing everything she could to get me through this time. *It's her time too*, I thought.

"Thank you for all you do, sweetie."

"You're welcome, hon . . . coffee?"

"Yes, please. You're the best!"

I do wish she'd tell me when there's a new gadget in the house that resembles a pistol, especially if she has to point it at my head. There's wisdom in that. I'll probably just keep that to myself.

But really, thank you, Lynn, for not snuffing me out in my sleep. Nice shot, though. I didn't feel a thing!

One Flu over the Coup Coup's Nest

I AWOKE WITH A bit of a runny nose and knew immediately what to do. Luckily, I had received the latest text from the Dept. of Nasal Sciences and was able to get the information I needed quickly. I called and was told there was a high volume of calls due to the recent increase in paranasal activity. I was quickly referred to the Dept. of Viral Influenza Protection and was informed that my call was important and that the wait would be approximately ten minutes.

Then it happened. I sneezed out loud! Alexa responded, "I have heard your violent reaction and am contacting local health officials." The air ambulance from the National Bureau of Health was there in record time, about eight minutes, I'd guess. Thank God we live close to the federal hospital. Time was of the essence in these emergencies. The taxpayer-funded helicopters were well worth the cost, for sure.

The Para sinus team entered quickly suited in full hazmat gear. They disarmed my home security in seconds with their emergency code. This wasn't possible before the coup. I was so glad they had that capability so that I didn't need to get up from the cot. They quickly started asking me questions to make sure I was still lucid, updating my records as I answered. They asked things like the date and time and who the current premier was. I really wasn't sure about the premier as they installed them so frequently. They nodded as if to say it was only a formality.

The one with the cellular transmitting device was in direct contact with the director of East Coast Membrane Desiccants who recommended a nasal swab and a medicated tissue product that would dry up the leaky nasal passage. A nostril trimmer/vacuum was then inserted to remove any rogue or elongated nostril hairs that might be retaining foreign particles. A measuring tool was then inserted to ensure proper hair length. That was a scary moment as I wasn't sure when I'd had my last trim. Fortunately, I was still within the parameters and wasn't immediately escorted to the Central Retraining Authority.

After a few minutes, calm was restored, and I was cleared by the Mucus Team lead. I was then given a Declaration of Awareness and instructed to use the medicated tissues three times a day for seven days. The "Dutifully Compliant" box was checked on the computer screen. That was a relief, for sure.

I thanked them for their excellent response and wished each of them an influenza-free day. I asked the one who appeared to be in charge who the new premier was because I really didn't know for sure. They all laughed together. Then, he told me it had been a bit of a trick question. "We always ask it as a security question to make sure the patient isn't one of us, a synthetic. Don't believe the news stories unless they are reported via PX (Putin/Xi, also known as "Putzie") International Media. They have a rating of 81-percent accuracy, you know."

"Yes, I know. It's nice to have the facts again!" I said, smiling.

He continued, "Surgeon General Antoinette Fauci's still premier. She's doing a great job. We haven't seen a full-blown threat since her grandad started the first Paranasal Investigation Unit."

"Things have gotten so much better since the coup," I responded. "I remember a time when I would have to buy my own tissues. I'd have to take the super train all the way to the Pharmaceutical Dispensary Station and even wipe my own nose!"

"Yes, ma'am. It was our pleasure." They exited via the open front door. "Can we help you with anything else today? No. Well then, we must be on our way. Remember to keep your nose clean. We don't want to have to come back."

"And you won't!" I smiled and pressed the key fob.

The look on their faces when the hypersonic phaser beams zapped them into oblivion was worth the years of research and development.

It was great to have another helicopter for the underground. We were advancing quickly. Synthetics would never understand their place. They still didn't know that our new Enigma7 machines translated the Russo-Mandarin slang they used as a programming language. They actually believed they understood espionage.

It's a good day to be human.

Billy the Kid

ANOTHER TRIP TO the doctor for some much-needed injections in my back. Please don't stop reading there. This isn't a complaint. It's kind of a "day in the life of an old guy making the best of a lousy situation."

By the time I get to the doctor, Lynn and I are both worn out. It's a hard trip because it's early and about an hour and a half drive, but it will offer me some relief until we can get to the point of consultation with a neurosurgeon, still days away. I have a few herniated discs in my lower back, five to be exact. It is debilitating, but we are in the system and looking forward to whatever options are available. The steroids help but can only be infrequently injected, so it's actually a blessing to receive them.

I enter the waiting room and fill out the required documents that state, "We [insert clinic] will not be held accountable if you fall off the table in your sedated state or try to tie your own shoes and are unable to avoid the swinging door or begin to drink out of the toilet or get hit by an asteroid." It's all there in the fine print.

The intake physician's assistant takes my blood pressure and begins the litany of questions that will guide his efforts to avoid the precarious conditions that occur in a seventy-year-old human body. Of course, I've already filled out that form, but for the sake of finding an error, he repeats the questions. I begin to think his side hustle must be as a fact-checker for some social media platform.

I never know when my inner child will burst into an ongoing conversation. It is the story of my life, and I am often entertained by the way he responds to questions. It's worse when I am tired or otherwise distracted. It's like being a part of a comedy team and the rest of the world is your straight man. The more serious the tone, the more outrageous the answers. It goes something like this:

Have you ever had GI issues?

Yes, I got an article 15 for a barroom fight when I was a GI in Germany, but that's been some forty years.

It takes him a minute, but he gets it. It's going downhill quickly. I can tell he knows it. He chuckles and tries to maintain his doctor composure because that's what the doctor's manual says, and he intends to be one someday, apparently.

"Have you recently had chemo?"

"Yes, I wear a chemoflaged hat sometimes, but today I'm wearing the DAWG hat because they just won the National Championship, so I thought it appropriate since most of you here went to Florida schools, and I wanted to rub it in a bit." I could see he found it difficult not to discuss football.

My blood pressure is somewhere around 600 over whatever, so he moves the cuff to the other arm. I've never understood this, but I'm sure it has to do with the fact that I'm probably ambidextrous and just never took the time to instruct the one side to read.

He goes down yet another list of ailments, which I answer quickly until he says, "Have you ever had a stroke or mini-stroke?" I wait several seconds and stare blindly to the front and act like I'm dozing. It takes him a while, but he gets that too. My wife has already caught onto the pattern. She's used to it. His student assistant clearly hasn't read the doctor's manual and bursts out laughing.

Now, I know I have the room. That's always a great feeling. He sticks the IV needle into the back of my hand, then squirts some liquid into the attached vial explaining to me that it is a saline solution. I have literally no option except to start singing "Sailing" (replacing the word with Saline) by Cristopher Cross. My wife giggles. She's in on it already, but now it's really on. There is no holding back the kid. Many have tried. It just won't happen.

Once they get a decent reading, 168 over something or other, the intake guy and his assistant leave the room, telling me it will be a few minutes. They are smiling, which meets the kid's approval.

They come to get me, so I hop on my trusty walker (which I have aptly named "Texas Ranger" in honor of Chuck Norris) and head to the room intended to look like an operating room on a smaller scale. I have to leave "Texas Ranger" outside the door as I will leave in a wheeled chariot pushed by a sober individual with a license to push them.

They try to help me onto the table and ask me if I can lie on my stomach. I say, "Sure, I can lie in any position. Ask anyone where I was on July 23, 1986." They begin to laugh and tell me just to get on my side. They ask if I have on loose underwear, so I tell them to ask my wife because she dresses me. The room appreciates the spirit. There is a young nursing assistant that helps me get onto my side. I explain that I have a hip that isn't my own and that the side I'm lying on is a bit uncomfortable.

One of the other assistants in the room states that they will start the medication shortly. I don't know what came over me, but the kid doesn't wind down just because medication is involved, so I begin to explain that I got the hip at a funeral home in South Florida from a guy named Walter L. Murphy or at least that was the name on the door. The outburst that followed caused them to momentarily suspend the procedure until they all ceased laughing. I was so proud. I continued with the fact that there were real bargains at funeral homes. I pointed to my dentures and said, "I got these for fifty bucks. All it took was a can of playdough, and they fit perfectly."

The nurse just couldn't contain herself, and I could hear the laughter from the staff behind me. As the room got calmer, the anesthesia guy (Gary) said he was starting sedation, to which I replied, "INCOMING," and that's all I remember. I woke up goofy with a blood pressure reading of 124 over who cares and got carted off to the car, still talking with dragons and swatting at the fairies who always show up to aggravate me when I'm in Nirvana.

It was good to entertain all the folks who work hard to keep us out of pain. I appreciate them all. I'm glad I could bring a little joy to their otherwise busy day. That inner kid makes me laugh too. His name is Billy. (My first name is William.) Billy the Kid. He keeps me sane in this unpredictable world! It's great to still have an imaginary friend after all these years, one who can turn tough times into brighter days.

Route 66

THE BIBLE IS my point of reference. I read it every day and hear or read topics or sermons on it every day and have for many years. I do that because it keeps me learning. I will forever be a Bible student. In it are not just words of wisdom but answers to complicated questions.

Many people use it like a fortune cookie and point out what the Bible says and what it doesn't. They try to make a case for themselves by trying to insert their own thinking into Bible discussions. That always shows.

The Bible doesn't have any trip wires. It does have mysteries and deep subjects that require discernment. That discernment comes from Holy God. We simply must read the Word and accept the interpretation of the Holy Spirit as it comes to us.

We, as Christians, have the same ability to discern as Matthew, Mark, Luke, and John. The indwelling Holy Spirit is the same Holy Spirit that dwelt in them. The words of the Bible are inspired by God himself. The indwelling Holy Spirit is the same Holy Spirit that inspired the writing in the first place. He is the one who teaches.

There are far more educated people than I. They have years of study and have come to a deeper understanding of context and matters that require spiritual discernment when it comes to what the Bible actually says and what it doesn't say. I will defer to them if my understanding is incomplete. I don't just randomly choose verses to shore up what I think. I have learned to think as

I am instructed from the words God has provided on the pages of the Bible.

I may not completely understand a particular subject, but you can be assured that I know the teacher, and I will allow him to correct me when I'm wrong, and He does.

If my insertion of the Bible offends you in any way, I can't really be sorry for that. Responding from the Word of God is the only way to settle moral questions, in my view. Quoting Scripture is not passing judgment. It is pointing to the truth as I know it.

I would love to retain all of my friends, but I can understand if you choose to take a different tack. The Bible isn't very popular these days. I get that. But I will study it and tell others about it because that is what God has prepared me to do.

James 4:17

So, whoever knows the right thing to do and fails to do it,
for him it is sin.

Heir Removal

So, You've got this idea to take prayer out of schools and public gatherings. Good luck with that. Parents now pray more for their kids than they ever did, as do churches and groups of people everywhere. God isn't bound by a building. As for the kids, which ones are praying? Yeah, but God knows, and He knows we're praying for your kids as well.

You want to remove Him from your money. Really? Why would He want to be on there in the first place? The love of money is "the root of all kinds of evil' (1 Tim. 6:10). I'd say scratch it off every time you see it. Just know that it's a reminder that God is far more powerful than anything you could buy or sell. God created the very idea of it!

You want to remove the cross from public view? Might I invite you to visit Arlington National Cemetery? Can't wait to watch you try that. We'll (gasp!) pray for you. Besides, if you'll notice, Jesus isn't on that cross. That's because he AROSE after being beaten and hung on it to die for you! Think about that. The cross is only a symbol of the price Jesus paid for you! How could you despise a symbol of that much love? Guess you like the little heart better?

You want to remove the name of Jesus from public prayer? How's that working out for ya? Thanks for calling attention to "the name above every name" (Phil. 2:9–11)! He knows who He is, and we know why you don't want to hear His name. There's power in that name, Jesus. There, I've said it!

Don't want to see a nativity, the manger, at Christmas? What are you thinking? Christmas is ABOUT the manger (Luke 2:1–20), the birth of Jesus (gasp again). Ask Santa Claus to help you when you're sick. See what he brings you, just sayin'.

You want to remove His name from your political party platform? Yeah, okay. "Boo" Him all you want. He has a long memory. Just know that it's a choice. I'm sure he'll be glad to NOT be associated with some of the things you do in His name.

The point is this: You can't remove Jesus from any place He wants to be. Jesus isn't just a name. He's a person, part of the Godhead bodily" (Col. 2:9). He is God in the flesh who died and rose again. How do you expect to remove Almighty God from anything? What twisted sense of outright pride makes you think you can make God disappear?

You see, God's "church" is God's people, and God said this" about His church: "No weapon formed against thee shall prosper" (Isa. 54:17). Basically, all your efforts will always be thwarted, maybe not in the moment but ultimately. You can build churches and organizations or anything you want that oppose God, but in the end, They will not prosper. God means what he says. You may disagree, but that won't change anything.

To end with a cliché, You may not believe in God, but He still believes in you, and you can't "remove" Him from anywhere He doesn't want to go. If you read all of this, God bless you. Have a conversation with Him right now. If you already know Him, pray for someone who doesn't!

War Lord

THE STATE OF the world is reason enough to look to heaven for answers. That much is obvious. Sometimes, though, I take the wrong tack and go about the business of trying to solve all the world's problems. In most cases, I find myself nothing more than a wet noodle in a boiling pot. Considering the multitude of problems present in the world, my own ability to engage in any activity outside of screaming into my pillow is quickly overshadowed by the certainty that I am overly taxed and far too involved with things that aren't mine to control.

Still, some days, I just have to go to war. This morning is one of those days. We're putting on the armor at my house and standing in the middle of all this madness. We're turning off the TV and making sure that our weapons are pointed in the right direction. We're taking our fighting positions.

Prayer requests are coming from everywhere. I seem to be feeling the world's pain today. I thank God for that kind of compassion. I haven't always had it, but I feel like I have to do something more, but something more is unnecessary.

I know exactly what to do, so I stop in the midst of all my own foolishness and deliver each request to the King. Family, friends, loved ones, and even enemies expect that of me. I feel compelled to join them in prayer. James 5:16 says, "Confess your faults one to another, and pray one for another, that ye may be healed. The effectual fervent prayer of a righteous man availeth much."

My own weakness becomes obvious. The world overwhelms me. It shouldn't if I trust God with the outcome. There are times when I have to gather my own burdens and those of my loved ones and place them all into the only hands that can actually do anything about anything. I have to understand and accept my place. It isn't my assignment to set it all straight. It is my job to dress for battle and humble myself before the King. Today, and every day, that is what I am required to do.

There is a disease out there, and it's making people very sick. If you don't know that, then you are sheltered from the truth. Whether you wear a mask or take the vaccine isn't the issue. It's all foolishness if we don't protect ourselves from the evil that wars against us. Do what you have to do, but I'm going to war. I'm putting on the armor and trusting God to do what He does. He is in the protection business.

The battleground is in the hearts and minds of people. I am reminded of my place in the war every day. Like everyone else, I am easily distracted, but not today! I have been assigned, as have all Christians, to fight the battles from our knees, to discern the spiritual and accept that we must get involved at the level from which we are most effective, where we can do the most good.

Compassion for others requires that we hold onto that thought, that we remain aware of the hurting, destitute, displaced, and the reality that every day, people need to know that we are engaged, praying for them without ceasing, prepared to face the devil himself if need be.

We are, in fact, the undefeatable army. However depleted we may appear, our power is still drawn from our omnipotent God! No weapon formed against us shall prosper. That means exactly what it says. No one can defeat the church that is God's people.

I'm also aware that the world doesn't get any better. It is the world in which many are unaware of the spirit that is consuming them. They only view their world on this earthly plane. The war is constant, and it is fought in a realm we can't really enter without choosing a side. I'm gonna stand on the side of Jesus. No other ground is safe.

"Ephesians 6:12 says, "For we wrestle not against flesh and blood, but against principalities, against powers, against the rulers of the darkness of this world, against spiritual wickedness in high places."

I am helpless to cure disease or cause armies to fall. I know that Jesus sits on the throne and that my one job is to appeal to Him on behalf of those too weak or distraught to make their own appeal. That is the battle to which we are all called.

My job is not to live in a world of "woe is me." Rather, it is to humbly seek the Lord's will in every matter. That is the perfect place for me. That is the whole of it, to place those I love and those within my reach into the hands of the only one who can show mercy and extend grace, not just because I ask but because He is righteous and holy. HIS grace is sufficient. His power is made perfect in weakness.

The war is ancient. It began in heaven and rages still. As with any war, it is necessary to find your place if you are to engage with the enemy. You really can't do that unless you are armed and ready for whatever the enemy launches at you. Know your real enemy. They won't speak of him on the nightly news.

If your only defense is to bellow and moan about the injustice of it all and protest man's inhumanity to man, then your cause is futile in the real war. Your satisfaction is neither guaranteed nor relevant to the real cause, which is to honor the King.

Romans 8:28 says, "And we know that all things work together for good to them that love God, to them who are the called according to his purpose."

If you want to engage the real enemy at the highest level, humble yourself before Almighty God and make your appeal to Him. That's the only way you can trust the outcome. I have to remind myself of that every single day. He is my advocate, and He loves me, always ensuring that His will serves a higher purpose than my own. He alone is worthy.

There is literally nothing to fear. The war has already been won. Jesus took our sins on the cross and crushed the evil that comes against each of us. The rest is well within His providence. Trust Him in everything.

Job 11:7–9

Can you find out the deep things of God? Can you find out the limit of the Almighty? It is higher than heaven—what can you do? Deeper than Sheol—what can you know? Its measure is longer than the earth and broader than the sea.

Globular Warning

YOU PROBABLY HAVEN'T heard any of this yet, but it's all hard-core science. I know that because people who know scientists told me it was. Only recently have reputable scientists in such fields as Washtub Imbalance Monitoring and Dreidel Physics been made aware of the devastating potential of an almost certain worldwide cataclysmic event.

Renowned globulist, Dr. Wonton Shupe of Wuhan/Harvard Association of Technical Utopian Predictors (WHATUP, a coop-erative education-sharing organization famous for their respective studies of viruses and other global disasters), states emphatically, "The total number of gravitons, while only hypothetical parti-cles, have been depleting due mainly to the number of people on the planet. In layman's terms, what that means is that the pull of gravity is being reduced with every person being born."

Together with other scientists of note (i.e., those applying for grants to study this phenomenon), consensus has been reached, maintaining that the effort to control the earth's spin is the most important endeavor of the twenty-first century, excluding, of course, efforts to fund the research to prevent mass destruction not yet discovered.

Manmade gravity depletion has begun to have tremendous effects on the earth's ability to rotate. The varying population migration throughout the world and the continued weight gain by those in the United States due to unprecedented COVID-related sheltering has caused a predictable wobble according to models. Senator Hank Johnson of Georgia confirms the modeling having had a similar experience concerning Guam and the near disappearance of that island due to overpopulation.

In most of history, the weight of humans has been offset by varying diets, resource development, and other ambiguous efforts, causing very little variance in the earth's stability. However, due to increased food supplies throughout the world, that balance has begun to cause a global wobble, which, in turn, could effectively cause the earth to spin completely off its axis.

Researchers at the Environmental Narrative Institute for Globular Magnetic Assimilation (ENIGMA) have long understood the potential of this disaster. A consensus of these scientists has estimated that humans will slowly begin to spin off the earth in less than five years. Globular slinging is not only possible but inevitable at this point. Already, small children and animals are disappearing off the face of the earth. The children and animals are our most precious resource. We must act quickly.

Dr Antonio Farchi, dean of Duke University's Predictable Environmental Disasters (D.U.P.E.D.) has declared the earth will be completely adrift and floating "somewhat like a ping pong ball in a tornado" within five years without certain precautions.

To combat the potential for global catastrophe, a "Sling tax" will be added to persons weighing under 150 pounds. For their own protection, children will be placed inside FEMA-approved portable glass domes. Visitation will be limited until indoctri . . . errr . . . training is complete.

Food production will be slowed worldwide in order to reduce weight gain and promote more healthy diets. Pizza and doughnuts, along with meat and potatoes, will be banned immediately. Weight gain will be monitored by IRS employees armed with medical warrants, and to coin a phrase, "Resistance is futile."

Those opting for the reinforced (Chinese) steel shoes to maximize gravitational pull will be allowed to purchase them through Amazon at a discounted rate for a short time. Small pets are at the greatest risk. Limit two sleeves per pet.

Jeff Bezos and Elon Musk have collaborated on the "Down to Earth" project that will ultimately redistribute the entire population of earth in a colossal effort to restore proper balance and reestablish new world order.

You will be notified via drone of your next station and mode of transportation.

Signed and sealed by unanimous declaration.

-Global United Establishment of Settled Science and the World Health Organization (GUESSWHO)

Self-Appointed

Guide: "I'm sorry, ma'am. You'll have to wear a mask to gain entry."

Woman: "But I'm dead. This is heaven. I thought . . ."

Guide: "Ma'am, the mask . . ."

Woman: "Okay, but you do know that it won't prevent anyone from getting whatever I have."

Guide: "Had. There's only one opinion that matters here, ma'am, and you're here because everyone comes here eventually. It's required."

Woman [donning mask]: "That's not what heaven is supposed to be about."

Guide: "Please enter the cubicle and await judgment. Jesus will see you shortly."

Woman: "Judgment? Doesn't the Bible say we aren't supposed to judge? This is ridiculous! First, the mask. Now a lockdown? You people really ought to—" [door closes. A few minutes pass.]

Guide: "Jesus will see you now. Please exit to the rear of the cubicle."

Woman: "Well, THAT took forever!" [escorted toward the light until Jesus comes into focus . . . faces throne.]

Jesus: "I'm not sure you understand the word forever."

Woman: "Good morning, Jesus. Good to finally meet you. May I remove the mask?"

Jesus: "No, the angels don't want what you have."

Woman: "But you're not wearing one, and why aren't they vaccinated?"

Jesus: "There is no vaccine for your disease. Besides, I'm God, and I'm asking the questions."

Woman: "Well, okay, but the optics—"

Jesus: "What makes you think you deserve entry?"

Woman: "I was a good mom mostly and a good wife, well, after I buried Alfred and the first one, what's his name . . . and I tried to keep everything around me organized. People are just so—"

Jesus: "But it never occurred to you to come to me or read about me in that Bible your mom gave you?"

Woman: "I never needed much help. I did everything. I thought that I needed to be independent and help others."

Jesus: "You could have helped more by being kind. I see you didn't attend church or worship in any way."

Woman: "I took the kids to Vacation Bible School and church camp once. As for church, it was just so . . . well . . . I never understood how it worked, and those people were so disorganized, and none of them could sing."

Jesus: "So, you opted to stay home rather than help. I had a job for you there."

Woman: "Well, I needed some 'me' time. The kids were crazy when they got out of school."

Jesus: "Why didn't you pray more?"

Woman: "Pray . . . Ha. . . I didn't think you'd hear me. You didn't listen when my mom died. How was I supposed to know when you listened and when you didn't?"

Jesus: "I always heard you, but you didn't hear me. Your mom is here. You didn't listen to her either. She prayed for you every day of your life."

Woman: "When do I see her?"

Jesus: "That's not how this works, Karen."

Karen: "What do you mean?"

Jesus: "You aren't staying."

Karen: "But that's not fair. I was a good—I always—I need to see the manager."

Jesus: "That won't work here, Karen. There is no higher authority."

Karen: "So I'm going to—"

Jesus: "Leave? Yes, because I never knew you."

Guide: "Please step toward the escalator."

Karen: "Don't touch me! I want to talk to this Satan person. Isn't he in charge down there?"

Guide: "He is for now. And he knows you're coming. You won't need the mask."

Karen: "Well, we'll have to see about that. There's no telling what diseases they have down there . . . and if you think for one minute, I'm going to—"

Karen can be heard shouting and making demands for only a few more moments as the escalator takes her down, out of earshot. The silence after her departure is deafening. Karen had finally spoken to the Manager.

Hebrews 9:27
It is appointed for men once to die, and after this the judgment.

Proverbs 21:2
A person may think their own ways are right, but the Lord weighs the heart.

High Tech

ALL INFORMATION HAS to go somewhere. What good does it do to know what size t-shirt I wear if you can't sell me another one when I need it? So, somewhere, the technology exists that not only knows what size t-shirt I wear but knows also what color choices I prefer and how best to get them to my door. That same technology knows where I live and what size pants I wear. The more I stay in my house and order products, the more "others" learn about me.

If I order drugs online, that same technology knows what conditions I take medication for and when and if they need to be refilled.

Technology knows my current financial status and my heirs. Technology knows who I would likely vote for and offers information that would favor one ideal or another. It is indeed manipulative.

The surreptitious nature of information gathering suggests that we don't have any idea what "they" don't know, nor do we know anything about "them."

The cancel culture is the new morality police. In essence, if you don't believe what they believe, you won't keep your job or buy and sell products that don't fall in line with whatever is the new, "accepted" criteria.

To date, there is no knowable force that protects privacy, nor is there a known collector. No one is accountable for invasions of that privacy from medical records to t-shirt sizes; there is an ongoing effort to know everything about everybody.

Technology has taken on a god-like intelligence without even a hint of accountability. That doesn't seem to concern the average American. They're too busy looking the other way and engaging in political infighting to be concerned about what they don't know.

I don't necessarily believe technology is the enemy, but I do believe protections are in order. "Know your enemy" is now a one-way street. They know you, but you don't know them. How then do you engage a potential threat that knows enough about you to literally disarm you before the battle begins?

For those who don't know God, there are no preventative measures that would allow them control over an ever-advancing invasion of personal privacy. The fear of Big Brother unnerves them. The power to oppose their bigger, more powerful, and all-knowing brother is, in truth, nonexistent.

But I know an omnipotent God who has power over all of that. I won't be canceled or otherwise restricted unless He allows it. That's why you can read this. There is wisdom in God's promise that He will never leave me nor forsake me. That wisdom replaces any perceived fear.

I don't have to spend my days concerned about what the data miners will find out about me next. I just know they are powerless against an omnipotent God. I needn't be concerned about the things of man if indeed I am seeking first the kingdom of God.

On this playground or any other, my Daddy is and will always be bigger than your daddy!

Psalm 27

Of David. The LORD is my light and my salvation—whom shall I fear? . . . Though an army besiege me, my heart will not fear; though war break out against me, even then will I be confident.

End of Days (The Broken Seal)

ONE FINAL ACT was all it took. The world crashed in that moment. I was immediately aware that a seal had been broken in heaven. I had studied these things and was somewhat well versed in the schedule of events that would surely follow.

I knew in that moment that the South would never rise again. I knew that America was broken and that the damage was irreparable. I knew that the world as we knew it, would come to a horrific end. The final insult had been issued.

There was a distant rumble when it happened. It sounded like it was moving toward us. Thunderous, almost growling winds gathered, probably protective angels running to the scene, but it was too late. The damage was done.

I started to shake, knowing the situation as I did. I began to pray out loud. Others joined in. They knew what was happening too. It was just so sudden.

Who knew the apocalypse would begin here at the Huddle House, known countywide for its friendly faces and omelets filled with meaty surprises, this one located in a small rural setting, still mostly protected from the real world?

The rumbling stopped as quickly as it began. Then came the sounds of a great wailing and gnashing of teeth. It isn't wise to interfere with warring angels.

I should have been more responsive, but the event was so surreal, I actually thought I must be having some sort of out-of-body experience, an observer in another realm, where good and evil war.

Looking back, though, I don't think I could have stopped it. It was as if it was all pre-destined like some prophesy that had to be fulfilled.

Had I been more aware, had any one of us in that room been suspecting in the least, we would have intervened. We would have recognized the call and answered as quickly as the heresy occurred. The gasps should have been enough to wake us.

We should have looked for the Jersey tags, but the car was backed into the parking space. We would have paid attention to that, but it was unremarkable, probably intentionally so.

I saw him reach for the pink Sweet n' Low packets. I never thought for a moment that he'd—it was over so quickly. He ripped open the packets and dumped them into his—I thought it was a mistake and he'd just inadvertently missed his coffee cup, but then he tasted it and added another packet.

That was the proverbial straw that broke the camel's back. That was the moment that loosed the hell hounds. That was the instant the clock struck midnight on Planet Earth.

I knew immediately that the demons had been released and that the final battle was soon to begin. I could almost hear the ancient battle cry.

It was as if he'd shaken his fist at the God of heaven and dared Him to respond. That answer will come quickly. There will be no place to hide. That much is certain!

Sweet 'n Low on grits . . . the final sacrilege.

Glimpse

WE WERE ON our retirement trip, the last leg of an East Coast-wide tour of New England that included a much-needed, post-covid visit with family and an amazing tour of America's history from Lexington, Massachusetts, to Gettysburg to the Civil War in the South, truly a bucket list trip for us.

It just came over me. I was on a riverboat, the Georgia Queen in Savannah, Georgia, having a great time watching much younger folks dance, listening to music from the seventies and just enjoying the scenery as it passed by the window. The rain was a bit lazy, enough to keep us inside for the first part of the cruise.

The rainy weather demanded coffee, so my wife went to the service bar to arrange for that to happen. I was left alone with my thoughts, seeing my own hazy reflection in the window like a hologram against the passing views of a few of my old haunts.

Then, it just happened. No particular song, no real reminiscing, no single event, or maybe all of that combined. It just happened. I don't remember ever having had this type of encounter . . . ever. It was the oddest, most awesome feeling. I can only describe it as suddenly repentant, grateful, and awed by God's presence, a virtual lightning strike of emotion and a presence that mere words could never explain.

My eyes welled up with tears, and I drew a deep breath as my entire life flashed before me. It was quick and sure, literally cutting through me like a surgeon's blade. I was aware of my transgressions but not burdened by them. I literally said these words as the thoughts raced through my head. "God, forgive me for my entire life." What I meant by that was that if I had missed confessing anything He remembered, just use this moment to forgive me, and He did right then, right there. I knew it immediately. Humbled doesn't begin to explain any part of the encounter.

I guess I'd been thinking about the times I'd been drinking with my Army buddies there on River Street and all the misdeeds and godless acts I had committed there so many years ago, but that was only part of it. There was a strange separation from those events as if I knew I had long since been forgiven. My heart bled, not in a sentimental or remorseful way; rather, in a victorious, defeating the devil himself kind of way.

There was the sudden exposure of my whole life and the sins I had committed. It wasn't just a moment of bearing the guilt of all of those experiences. It was a sudden and overwhelming understanding of forgiveness. I forgave everyone who had ever wronged me. I realized the necessity of that as I became deeply repentant for my own transgressions against others and Almighty God, Himself.

There is no explanation beyond these words. The God of the universe forgave my sins through His only Son, Jesus. I was indeed a sinner, saved by grace through faith in Jesus.

These weren't just words any longer. My experience was a gift from a holy God that was unique in its presentation. There was a certainty, an assurance that I was forgiven, as if something was lacking and was now being acknowledged. I really wanted to engage with the Lord in this moment, but it was only a lingering breath, literally short and sweet. I was instantly prayerful and aware that mercy and grace were in the room. Not only was I forgiven but I was comforted by that act.

I am the only one who could understand the complexity of it because it was personal, and certainly only God could forgive me for my youthful indiscretions, not to mention my adult wandering. What I was experiencing was a fleeting yet eternal moment when God Himself just walks into a room and tears open a man's heart. I knew beyond any shadow of a doubt that I was forgiven, completely and totally. It was indeed a moment I can never forget and one that strengthens my faith to the point of being comfortable with my inheritance. Heaven is in my future. "What a day of rejoicing that will be."

What I experienced was a moment of sincere gratitude. There is nothing that explains a grateful heart. I was alone in a room full of people having a moment with God Himself.

The tears welled and leaked out briefly because they had nowhere else to go. I trembled a bit, and I knew that instant that I was forgiven. That's not a minor event. It is comforting beyond what you might think. There is a peace to it that is indeed beyond understanding. I guess I had been seeking that beyond even my own ability to ask. It was, I believe, one of the "desires of my heart" as the Bible so aptly refers to it.

Of course, these are all just words to describe an event that happened in a place called eternity because no earthly place can accommodate it. It was brief, and I only caught a glimpse, but I can say that I could have died in that moment and walked right on into heaven. I was so affirmed and comforted by the thought of complete forgiveness that nothing could interfere with the ongoing sense that the burdens of my heart were literally "rolled away."

I took off my glasses and wiped the fog away. I was sure no one noticed, not that I would have cared. I had been graced with an eternal presence. It was a moment between me and the living God of the ages. It came without warning or fanfare. There was no prompting, no song that reminded me, and no memory that was suddenly exposed. There was just me and the Lord and an over- whelming communication from Him…to me!

The reason I'm even attempting to explain this encounter is to try to relate a remarkable event in my life defined in earthly terms as a brief moment when all of heaven opened up, and I was suddenly relieved of a burden I didn't even know I was carrying. I also wanted to mark the experience as something personal and com- pletely supernatural if that word can be used to properly explain the experience.

Then there's this: God can walk into any room, any time, and open a heart. He isn't shy. He needs no introduction. He's Almighty God. He has an open invitation. He can perform the surgery you require without leaving a scar, instantly! He can leave as fast as He entered because He's not bound by time. He can linger if He wants, but you'll know. You'll just know. There's no mistaking His presence.

My wife came back with the coffee, and I didn't utter a word about what had happened until later that night. I briefly tried to explain it, but it wasn't something that could be restored to its original glory. The words weren't there because there was only one word that could describe the moment.

Hallelujah!

I sure hope you have this moment, the unmistakable reality of forgiveness beyond anything you might imagine. God is who He says He is. Forgiveness is inexplicable but certainly a great gift from God. Forgive others. You'll be amazed at what can happen.

Mark 11:25

And when you stand praying, if you hold anything against anyone, forgive them, so that your Father in heaven may forgive you your sins.

Lights Out

UNTIL THAT MOMENT, the only part of the Cold War I'd experienced was the cold part. I'd seen nothing but cold weather and constant field maneuvers for months at a time. I had visited the local towns briefly and was somewhat acquainted with the customs, but mostly I had become enslaved to the Army that had brought me so far. One more event, and I'd have a little more time to explore my new home. I fully intended to taste the exquisite food and enjoy the uniquely crafted beer that was my initial reason for picking this particular duty station.

In or around January 1981, I was a participant in a ground exercise in Coburg, West Germany, before the Berlin Wall came down. I remember it was an unusually cold night. We were gathered in a small, tower-like structure at a place we called Neustadt Mountain, overlooking Sonnenberg, East Germany.

I was new to the exercise. It was, to me, just another observation point to guard, repeat my general orders, and keep a lookout for jeeps that might deliver the Officer of the Day. I was a soldier in a much bigger operation, one that required me to spend the night posting guards at the 1K Zone, making sure none of the lesser-ranked imbeciles froze to death or got their tongues stuck to their gun barrels.

Our radar and other equipment were set up in a small room with large, unobstructed windows, monitoring movements on the eastern side of the border. This was an every-night affair, but it was all new to me.

I found it all very interesting. I was not really a student of inter-national affairs. I was just a soldier, fulfilling my obligation to my country, unaware of the politics and delicate balances that required my presence in the first place.

It felt like a spy movie. My buddies were unusually ordered. Everyone was busy and exceptionally quiet. There were two men listening through headphones and charting activity. They were the reason for the quiet. I was the only one who associated the entire scene with a book I'd read as a kid. It was literally "all quiet on the Western front." I kept that to myself.

It happened as quickly as you'd imagine as if someone just flipped a switch. All the lights went off in the town. Sonnenberg went dark.

It took me by surprise, and I just stood there staring, wondering if something had happened that had taken out the entire grid. I actu-ally muttered the question, "What the heck was that?"

I remember one of my friends who regularly visited the listening post said simply, "Welcome to communism." He then explained that the power on the eastern side of the wall was turned off each night at 10:00 p.m. I kind of shook my head in disbelief. I couldn't imagine how so many people would give way to some distant order. How could they allow someone to just extinguish their light and heat?

In my naiveté, I remember thinking how cruel that was to force people into darkness on such a cold night. I could not imagine why they would allow such a thing. I wondered what monster could cause so many to have to resort to other methods of heating their homes and feeding their families.

I began to understand that someone had actually pulled the switch by order of another higher-up who had supervised the blackout and another above him and so on up the ladder to a place where the order was given. It seemed to me that there was control beyond anything I could actually sort out. How could people allow this to happen?

I was, of course, an American, unusually privileged and free because our American system wouldn't allow for anything of this sort. Our people would rise up and squelch any such action. That was who we were. That was what we stood for, and that was exactly what I was there to prevent. It made me kind of proud, for the moment, at least.

That was the first time I felt the hot breath of the monster. I was literally in his den. I remember the sudden stench and gut-wrenching feeling that he'd be around long after I was gone. We'd need to continue our exercise and watch this mind-controlling devil.

Now, years later, I am beginning to smell the stench again. I'm not as innocent as I once was. I know that there's a monster on the loose. We see and hear his movement, yet we ignore his actions. He's roaming the globe, entrenching himself in the systems that control the people. He's in our house. He's under our beds. We ignore his sour breath. We pay no attention to his ancient call. We literally feed him from our own trough. We won't believe it until the switch is pulled and the lights go out.

That is the way of this communism. The monster that controls it is cunning and powerful. He takes what he wants because he is allowed.

1 Peter 5:8

Be sober, be vigilant, because your adversary the devil walketh about as a roaring lion, seeking whom he may devour.

Time-Bombed

I NEVER ASK, "WHERE did the time go?" because most of the time, I know. I abused it. I was inattentive to the gift, unconcerned with the value of it, ungrateful for the possibilities attached to it, and certainly unwise in my use of it.

As a steward of all that God gives me, it seems that I am most selfish with my time. I know I certainly don't spend enough time with the Him, which has an effect on everything else I do. He alone is in charge of its distribution. He, the arbiter of its worth.

It seems I am bound by time rather than focused on eternity, trying to get everything done, hurrying to accomplish all the tasks, make all the appointments, and "finish" all the projects, ignoring the purpose God has for me, delaying the very moments I should be spending with Him.

. . . worshiping . . . praying . . . listening.

If I intend to resolve to do anything within the confines of the time I am allotted, I resolve that I will spend more time with the Lord, as it is the most precious, most productive, and most perfect use of the time He has given me.

I don't intend to "make more time" for Him, as he is the sole creator of it. Rather, I will spend more of the time He gives me in His company, reading His Word, and listening to His voice. He alone is worthy!

Matthew 6:33

But seek first the kingdom of God and his righteousness, and all these things will be added to you.

A Matter of Decorum

WITHOUT IT, CIVILITY becomes a sign of weakness but only to the weak. Those who don't possess it or even attempt to employ it are without defense. The rest are simply observers looking for a proper invitation. There is an actual sense of decorum, though we may sometimes lose it somewhere between our frustration and outrage.

There is a difference in political correctness and decorum. Because some actions are unacceptable to the sensitive few doesn't mean we should refuse to be polite. One is a matter of restraint, the other a matter of upbringing. But there are limits to even the most docile practitioner.

Cursing in public generally comes from a place of ignorance or just downright meanness. Some people didn't have a mama. That's immediately detectable in their speech.

Bobbie Elizabeth was my mother. She was as sweet a woman as you could imagine. She was indeed polite company. She loved to have folks over for coffee and would sometimes even bring out the store-bought oatmeal cookies, probably because my dad loved them and bought them for himself. He would share them with us, but my mother didn't want him gaining any advantage, so she offered them to anyone she entertained.

Bobbie understood cussing. (Not to be confused with cursing, an altogether different practice.) It was a weapon for her. My father had no understanding of it and was embarrassed by its use. His father was a preacher. His mother a piano player at their church. They didn't curse . . . period!

My mom was raised by a half-Cherokee Indian mother and another half-Cherokee father who had a fondness for firewater up until the time he gave his life to the Lord. Unfortunately, her formative years were during the time of his relentless pursuit of the bottle. So, she learned the language of too much alcohol and how to speak fluently in the language of drunken cussing. Hers was a refined copy but deadly when called upon. I would liken it to a superpower.

She was beautiful . . . Scarlet O'Hara beautiful. Even I was forced, at times, to confront the men who would ogle her when we were in public. I became adept at coming between them and her, staring back until they averted their eyes.

She ignored their advances, but I'm sure she secretly knew the power she possessed.

Raven hair, deep blue eyes that twitched when she was angry, and a penchant for swishing when she shouldn't. I came to understand that what others viewed as "prissing" was actually a bad foot. She'd learned to use it to her advantage. She had a way of overcoming any disadvantage. She was blessed, to say the least.

On occasion, she wore red lipstick because there weren't too many other colors from which to choose. She didn't overdo it, but any effort to enhance her already naturally beautiful features was considered "too much" by those who were blessed with so little. The jealous others were her natural enemy.

Most women despised her, usually because their husbands couldn't keep their glances to a minimum. She really was beautiful. My sister and I could actually laugh at the bumbling men who would try to get her attention. She could look right through them or past them as the need arose.

Once, at a furniture store owned by our neighbor and friend, one of these self-styled suitors went a bit too far with his advances. I was about ten or thereabout. I'm not sure exactly, but I remember calling the man a name that questioned the marital status of his parents. It was an unwelcome defense.

I didn't see it coming, but my mother came around with a right hand that walloped me nearly to the ground. I guess that my defense of her had been a tad overly ambitious. I was not allowed to disrespect my elders, no matter what!

The man responded with a "That'll teach ya." That immediately infuriated my mother. That's when the hammer fell. She went into a place few in that day had ever witnessed. Think Sodom and Gomorrah or maybe Hiroshima. To put it mildly, she morphed into something completely foreign to my sister and me. We'd seen her angry before, but not like this.

She rushed the man and got right into his face. He was a burly type and made an effort to laugh her off, which further infuriated her. I didn't think that was possible. Her eyes began to twitch.

There weren't many folks in the store, but those who were there turned toward the brawl. It escalated quickly and just as quickly became a brutally one-sided verbal whoopin'! I couldn't hear her at first, but her voice kept rising to a place that was disturbing, not shrill but rather a roar. Apparently, this man had tried to engage her before.

She started with the fact that she knew his wife and that he should be embarrassed by his own inability to control himself. Then she went after him in a very personal way, to and including his obese build and what she termed his "obnoxious Yankee tone." She explained in no uncertain terms that the store was owned by a friend of hers and that she didn't come in to listen to his catcalls from the streets of New York.

He started to back away and tried to get her to calm down, at which point she buried what was left of her anger into a place I'll never forget! It was an "if you ever" with consequences ending in my father's presence and the end of a gun barrel.

She inserted expletives so precisely that I had a hard time believing she hadn't planned the encounter. She was mostly damning him to the nether regions and referring to him as less than adult and certainly lacking in social graces. It ended with "These are my children" and a final "How dare you!" that echoes in my memory almost every day.

Until much later (we knew better than to say a word), my sister and I had no idea that what we had witnessed was the epitome of a mother's love in the defense of her children and the fury of a scorned woman. We just thought she was awesome! It was worth the cold, hard punishment I had received.

She left the store and apologized for nothing! Bobbie Elizabeth didn't apologize!

Damn, I loved that woman!

What Choice Do I have?

TODAY, I WILL walk to the living room of my home. It won't be pain-free just yet, but the movement will be a miracle of science, likely not possible fifty years ago. Recent complications have made it necessary for me to use a walking machine designed by folks who cared enough to provide mobility assistance to those with disabilities. I am temporarily disabled, so I appreciate the work. I recognize the convenience and value of this machine. I believe it to be an engineering marvel.

I also believe that learned doctors using the latest technological advancements performed a medical miracle on my body. The various means, tools, medicines, and procedures, all are literally scientific wonders. It is truly amazing to behold the wonders of science.

I believe in that science brought about by men and women who, by virtue of their brilliant minds and caring hearts, take on the pain of others. People who design and build machines that bring comfort to those who are less fortunate than others are remarkable beings themselves. They are constantly in the world as if created to fill the void of those who came before them, advancing the causes of science.

However, the moment I see the light on the curtains in the morning, I step out onto the porch and feel the crisp air that nips at my skin and tells me there is still a touch of cool in the southern air. In that moment, I will take in the panoramic view of a well-tamed and finely tuned marvel that I believe was created and set into motion by God Himself. That's when the sun explodes!

I look across a lake brimming with aquatic life. I watch graceful herons gliding by, momentarily silhouetting themselves against a slowly bluing sky. The Spanish moss sways gently. The various flora and fauna appear. Birds of prey sneak over the water hunting for their breakfast, their young screaming from the trees. Songbirds flit about announcing the birth of another day as if it were the only one that ever mattered, all operating within the boundaries of an ever-involved Creator.

I will watch for a few moments as the bright yellow globe creeps over the eastern tree line, painting the grey sky with a light blue brush, and splashing color on the lake as it reflects what God Himself has painted. The earth spins because He commands it. Nothing else explains it.

I inhale the beauty and bow my head to reverence my God who creates it all, even the moment. I accept that He has made it all. I give Him the glory and thank Him for it. The whole of it moves in waves. Breezes blow, reeds bend, and leaves shuffle across softly swirling sand. It is Almighty God announcing His presence, whispering to every creature, giving them purpose.

At this moment, when all of nature awakens, I am at peace with the God of creation. There is no choice to make. I do not wonder what science this is or how it works. I am comfortable in this place of new creation because I can watch it washing away the darkness. I can feel my soul being cleansed as I worship a holy God.

I have no decision to make. It isn't a matter of choice for me. I can see it all for myself. Science works within the boundaries set forth by the Creator of everything. God is who He says He is. Science cannot replace God. It can only work within the confines of His providence. Science cannot offer me the advantage of eternity.

Job 38:4–7

Where were you when I laid the earth's foundation? Tell me, if you understand.
Who marked off its dimensions? Surely you know! Who stretched a measuring line across it? On what were its footings set, or who laid its cornerstone—
while the morning stars sang together and all the angels shouted for joy?

Bandits

I DON'T KNOW HOW they do it. I'm sitting here drinking my coffee. It's a beautiful morning. It's early. All is right with the world, thinking about nothing, and here they come.

It starts with a couple of herons drifting over to their hunting grounds. Then there's a splash. Suddenly, there's more of them lined up to stab a meal at the Shallows Bait Store, hammering away at the shad, being picky even. I watch them for a minute, maybe a bit longer. They gather and decide which ones will silhouette themselves against the sun after breakfast.

I see that pesky armadillo waddling by, using the tree line as his compass. I dare him to burrow, but he doesn't. He just makes his way to the drainpipe. I think about the last time he came this way. He remembers it too. We coexist by virtue of his underground lifestyle and my ability to track him. I watch till he's back into the wetlands where he belongs.

Then, without a hint of warning, an osprey literally nosedives into the cove from the treetops. He comes up with a fish and heads over to the nest where the family shouts approval at the sight of their still squirming breakfast.

Having dutifully fed the ungrateful brood, he soars away, hunting for more. His screams pierce the quiet; sharp, syncopated, echoing through the wetlands and across the lake. It's his victory cry. His family doesn't care. He screams anyway. He's doing his job, and he wants everyone to know it!

The hawk sails by, graceful as a swan but deadlier than a bolt of lightning. If I didn't know better, I'd think he was toying with his prey. I see what he sees and, sure enough, there's an empty mound where a frog used to be.

I grab my camera phone and take a few shots against a sky now slathered with a butter-colored paste. It all melts together. Everything flies and slithers and swoops and burrows, diverting my attention and stealing my time. I don't know how they do it. It's as if they plan a new episode every morning, one that will divert my attention from my work.

Sooner than I expect, it's an hour later, sometimes two. I head to the kitchen to make coffee. She's already there making coffee. I prepared it last night, but we have to hit the buttons each morning. We share a grumbly good morning and fill our mugs with the Columbian concoction. I pour hers because her hands are sore. We sit in the living room and say nothing because words are completely unnecessary.

We allow the bandits to steal a few more minutes as we sip and stare and watch the water glimmer and sparkle just before the sweltering heat takes the morning's breath away.

It's summer on Crescent Lake. These ever-lovin' bandits have stolen another morning, or did I just let them have it?

Romans 13:12

The night is almost gone, and the day is near. Therefore, let us lay aside the deeds of darkness and put on the armor of light.

Writing the Wrong

I COULD CALL THIS "A Message from My Sponsor," but it is a necessary discussion I like to have from time to time in an effort to offer clarity to those who read my somewhat lengthy stories. Sometimes the words have to be deeper than normal, but it's hard to go deeper.

I try to tell the story of my own salvation in an effort to encourage others. If you are reading this, I have no other message beyond the necessity for a Savior and that I have indeed given my life over to Him, choosing every day to serve His purposes by writing these brief interludes. That alone does not absolve me of my sin. Only Jesus can do that.

If there is a single theme to my writing, it is this: that Jesus is who He claims to be and that He alone is the way, the truth, and the life, just as He claims. Many want to relegate that conversation to one of comparative religions or meaningless details written by philosophers and others who find purpose in questioning the very idea of eternity. Those are the ideas on which the worldly stand in order to claim their independence from any power that might be greater than themselves. I'd be completely foolish to accept that those who believe differently than I will somehow be converted because of these scribblings. My effort here is only to plant a seed. I cannot conduct any business beyond that. There just isn't room or time for the back and forth.

Sometimes I write about my personal experiences, but that requires me to explain the depths to which I had sinned in my own life. I don't necessarily like to discuss those things. No one does. The reason I don't like to do that is because it turns into a competition about who might be the most sinful, which is never a cause for explanation since, indeed, we are all sinners, and all fall short of the glory of God, myself included. The wages of that sin is death, something else we will all ultimately experience.

There is no need to tell my story beyond the fact that I have been forgiven. I will, if called upon to do so, but this isn't an arena that allows that in one fell swoop. Suffice to say, I am a sinner. I struggled with sin, not the depth of it but the fact of it. I was guilty as charged. I knew that. I was convicted of it. Whether I was spitting on the sidewalk or robbing a bank doesn't matter. I sinned against God.

That seems to be the place where most people tend to defend their position or launch their attack. That, too, is a questionable response because I have no power nor any ability to judge your sin. That, too, is far above my paygrade.

I have sins of my own. That is the point where we can connect. That is the level playing field on which we must all stand. I stand in a place of having been found guilty. I invite you to that ground. You may or may not see it my way, but I can assure you that I am not going to budge from that position. I have been forgiven by the only one who can forgive my sins.

That is the central theme for any message written to those who find themselves searching for answers to the debilitating consequence of life's struggles. I could relate those sins that would declare my exceptionally bad behavior, but it is important to extend that conversation to what can be done about it. Living a good life isn't the answer, nor will it launch you or me into heaven. There is only one place of complete forgiveness and one way to enter heaven.

The level of our personal sin is irrelevant. The most important detail about that sin is that we all—every single one of us—have need of a Savior. Our sin is against God. He alone has the power to forgive that sin. He does so completely, permanently, and eternally. Think on that.

We tend to dismiss the thought of eternal punishment and accept, to some degree, the idea of eternal bliss or "resting in peace" when we die. Ignoring the idea of a just God who punishes sin just isn't on the menu. There is biblical evidence for eternal peace and eternal punishment. The problem is that we cannot accept that God is as just as He is loving. It's like we can't be charged if we aren't guilty. Yet, we are all guilty.

No matter how I write that, it offers the same conclusion, which is this: Jesus saves. Of course, sharing this would serve a purpose. Maybe it will cause someone to think or look up during a difficult time. That is the only hope we have in anything we do. Pray that this lands on the right heart!

These two verses are something we should all use to encourage one another. God wants to speak with us and reason with us.

Isaiah 1:18

"Come now, and let us reason together," says the Lord, "Though your sins are like scarlet, they shall be as white as snow; though they are red like crimson, they shall be as wool."

1 John 1:9

If we confess our sins, He is faithful and just to forgive us our sins and to cleanse us from all unrighteousness.

Letters from Dad

I HAVE FRIENDS WITH enough letters by their names that they actually leave some of them off in order to appear real. Some of them are so well educated that they literally cannot visit earth without a sedative. Engaging with them in conversation is difficult but not impossible. The really bright ones know that they are set apart somehow and are blessed to breathe in the rarified air in which they walk. They are hardly pretentious. They realize not just the privilege of their education but the gifting of the ability to learn beyond the normal scope of the general population. I can say that they see things differently, not with elitist intent, rather devoid of simplicity. Complication is their friend. I am not of this ilk.

They work very hard to do the things that I find easy, like having a conversation. You can tell it's hard for them, and I always appreciate that they can bring it down a few notches and talk about the world from their perspective. I enjoy their company and understanding of the world. It is how I gain understanding of how they think and why our thinking is different. It never boils down to their level of education. It always comes down to sources. The Bible is mine. I try not to wield it like a hammer.

There was a time when I wanted to pursue such an education, but I was not inclined to study, and I didn't exactly apply what I learned to living a life separated from the world. In fact, I ran after it. To say I was worldly would be a bit of an understatement, but I would have liked to have had something besides my name if only to give me credentials.

My father finished the tenth grade and went into the service to fight a war even though his brothers were already there. He joined at seventeen, and being the youngest of six brothers, was kept stateside due to the Sullivan rule. He worked on airplanes and did his duty. That was the kind of man he was. He went to work in the Bell telephone system after the war. He struggled to achieve there due to his lack of formal education but did eventually rise to a management position. He retired after over thirty-five years and lived comfortably until his passing a few years ago.

My dad studied the Bible. He studied with a passion most people wouldn't understand. His father was a Bible teacher and preacher. My dad followed in his footsteps. He studied it all his life. He was tough on me, but he took me to church and helped me in ways that would cause me to always reflect on his teaching. I was a problem child out of the chute. He was impatient with me but deliberately so. We became friends much later in life, only after my decision to settle into my own skin and became somewhat receptive to a much-needed course correction.

One Sunday morning, at the request of his pastor, a gentleman with a lot of letters at the end of his name, attended my dad's Sunday school class. He had heard that my dad was a very good teacher. He was also the president of a Baptist seminary. His name was Dr. John Studor, an absolutely brilliant theologian. He and my dad had deep discussions about theology. I know because I heard them and learned from them. They became very good friends.

For years, they talked and discussed and sometimes would even disagree. My dad would always stand his ground and was some-times able to sway the opinion of the doctor, or at least present a good case for his perspective. He was always receptive to the doctor's guidance as well.

One day, Dr. Studor came to my dad's house for coffee, as he often did. He brought a group of men who sat with him in the living room and discussed many different doctrines of the Bible. They spent a lot of time sewing it all together. It was a contextual discussion of considerable depth. My dad was unusually confident but selective in his speech. One of them was the dean of the seminary, another was chairman of the board of trustees of the seminary—men of admirable status in that day. These men were there to offer him something he didn't even know he was pursuing. They were going to give him an oral examination, and if he passed, he would have conferred upon him the title doctor of religious education. This introduction was a precursor to what followed.

My dad began to study diligently as the day of his testing approached. I remember during those days when I would come to visit him, he would come out of his den with a furrowed brow and have what seemed to be an obligatory conversation with me as if he were preoccupied. I realized he was deep into his study and prayerfully approaching the Author of it, so much so that he would hardly speak at dinner.

Then, one morning he called and told me that I could refer to him as "Doctor" if I was so inclined. He was, to say the least, excited that he would be putting on his first cap and gown and receiving an honorary degree in religious education, which meant that not only was he well studied but he was affirmed in teaching the theology he so enjoyed. It wasn't just honorary, though. It wasn't a gift at all. It was the result of years of dedicated study. As we saw it, he was taught by the best Professor available. The Holy Spirit will do that. I watched and listened to him on more than one occasion give counsel to folks who asked. He was quick with answers and filled with wisdom. I, too, received that counsel. He would go to great lengths to answer questions.

He was the most educated man I ever knew, humble in some ways but confident in most every setting. He was able to give the "whole counsel" of God in virtually any circumstance, it seemed. I respected him more than any man walking. The day he left to be with Jesus wasn't necessarily sad for me. There was loss, of course, but I was able to walk through it without too much grief and experience a peace that couldn't be explained. That, too, was a gift from the Holy Spirit of God. My dad had taught me about this, and I knew it was as it should be. I knew exactly where he was and knew I would see him soon enough. He was my dad, friend, teacher, and mentor.

His birthday is coming up, and I swell with pride when I think of him. He was a remarkable man. I still try to make him proud by using the letters he gave me to put beside my name. I use them when I write and expose them whenever I am able to speak on the things of God.

My name is Stan Drew **Jr.**, and I pride myself in those letters after my name.

Arrested Development

I USUALLY DON'T CONCERN myself with my own level of mastery regarding the aging process, but wisdom requires me, at times, to review the hard lessons I've learned. I then pretend I understand the value of them. Otherwise, aging has no purpose beyond repetitive foolishness. So, a brief review is sometimes in order. I tell myself to remember these things as I move toward the light. Hopefully, I'll realize the lights are from oncoming vehicles, and I should step out of the traffic before the ambulance driver hears the second thump. So, here's a brief review. I'm all about helping others, so take note of these and learn from my mistakes.

Lesson #1) Don't eat that. When you're young, you can test your gastrointestinal limits. That all changes when you come to be a gentleperson of a certain age. Most cereal and other fillers are inherently explosive when mixed with fiber like Metamucil or Cheerios. You're old enough to know better. Try not to scare the children. They don't want to pull your finger. Remember the last time.

Lesson #2) Don't say that. Certain words identify you as an older (intestinal gas)."Holy Mackerel," "Bejesus," "Spiffy," "Giterdun," and "Kwitcherbellyachin" are all antique words, and please, no more "Groovy." Just stop, and by the way, "Dagnabit," "Fudge," "Shipapotomas," and "Sons of my Britches" are not proper cuss-words. You're not fooling anybody. It's better to ask forgiveness than to try to scream alternative curse words at the coffee table.

Lesson #3) Don't refer to these people. They're mostly dead. The Rolling Stones have been in various stages of death for some thirty years. Because they still perform is nothing more than a reenactment. They should be referenced as historical figures when discussing music. Dick Clark lived at least fourteen centuries before Kiss, and they're in their seventies. Neither are remembered as historic figures beyond music. Dick passed a decade ago at age eighty-two, along with Porky Pig (eighty-seven) and Wiley Coyote (eighty-five). Bart Simpson is forty-two, for heaven's sake, and Madonna (sixty-three) is old enough to draw Social Security. Google that if you must.

Lesson #4) Don't think that. The moon landing happened. It's not Tuesday yet, so no, don't take those pills, and stop mashing the brakes on the passenger side of the car. There's a reason people drive you around. Don't think you can swim. Refusing the flotation device is like playing clarinet on the Titanic. Finally, don't get your head sunburned. Not wearing a hat turns your scalp into bacon.

Lesson #5) Don't dance in public. This wasn't a problem before everyone had a camera, but now you run the risk of becoming a meme, which makes the rest of us look like Elaine from Seinfeld or worse. It's not just that. It's okay to dance in private, but you have to remember you did the Twist and the Frug and, for cryin' out loud, the Bump! That hip doesn't have a warranty.

Lesson #6) Don't jump off of that! Stepping off the bottom step shattered your ankle. Parking too close to the curb ruined your knee. Why would you even consider jumping across that puddle? You're already slowly beginning to bend closer to the ground. You're not friends with the physical therapy people just because they call you by your first name.

Lesson #7) Don't deny that. You were that stupid. You climbed up on the billboard sign and did the tomahawk chop for the news cameras. That would have been okay considering the Braves were going to the World Series for the first time, but then you decided to be famous. Just remember that emptying your bladder from a great height in Atlanta (Buckhead) traffic made you a criminal. Try to remember that!

Lesson #8) Don't wear that. It needs to be thrown out. That alligator on your golf shirt was popular back when Members Only was dating London Fog. It literally screams Boomer! Don't let them talk you out of your cargo shorts or New Balance sneakers. These are staple items for the unbalanced and those who don't have purses.

Lesson #9) Don't assume. Never ask how the pregnancy is going or who's the dad, not even in church. Make sentences without pronouns. Use y'all and try not to use conservative terms like liberty and America. Don't start none. There won't be none.

Lesson #10) Lastly, you don't understand women. Don't even lean in that direction. Continue to nod in their presence. Smile when you say stuff and fix what you can. Don't open their doors or pretend to have an opinion that doesn't mirror theirs. The garbage is going to overflow. Take it out without comment. You will make mistakes. Apologize. The biscuits will see you through. It's a process. Live with it.

Hope this helps. I'm still not sure I'm doing any of this right.

Klandestine

HERE I WAS, headed to church. I waved at a young neighbor at the corner. I rolled down the window, said good morning, and asked about his family. I had heard they were sick. I casually mentioned I was going to church and that we would pray for them. He was immediately unnerved and turned that rather unremarkable conversation into a pulpit for his own sermon.

In his brief rejection of the idea of attending church, he laughingly referred to the meeting as a meeting of white supremacists going about the business of planning more conspiracy theories, using God as their excuse. I wondered if he had ever even been to church.

I was a bit taken aback but not so much as to be unkind. I decided to "virtue signal" rather than argue a mindless accusation because that is what a display of kindness is called among his radical group.

Apparently, I was out to plan some sort of attack on those who had different sexual appetites and, of course, those who believed that women shouldn't have a choice in childbirth. There could be no other reason why I would attend church regularly because no God would support that kind of thinking. I listened rather than incited the already volatile reaction, especially with a talking billboard for propaganda.

I dared not suggest that I might be congregating with other like-minded people and worship as I was allowed. Having never met him, I just casually nodded and showed no fear of his bullet point-a-thon because there wasn't an ounce of interest in a response. He asked if we would be burning any crosses. I told him that wasn't likely.

I assured him that the meeting would be diverse and that we would, as usual, be discussing the things of God. I invited him to attend again just as a matter of defiance, but he adamantly refused because he said that he feared there would be too many weapons there and that everyone would misidentify him and call "him" by improper pronouns. I told him that the congregation wouldn't do that intentionally, but he needn't be offended if they did.

That was all it took to send him off on a rampage that included all Christians' intent to cram their Bibles down everyone's throat and demand that the world cater to their beliefs and that they are somehow above all the madness and that the "privileged" had caused the rest of the world so much pain. I tried not to show any signs that he was affecting me.

I said to him simply that I was going to church and that he was welcome to come and see what all the fuss was about.

"Not on your life! I've seen what happens to Christians. I've seen on TV that there's a place in Africa where they are killed every day. Why would I join them?"

"My answer was simply, "You should ask yourself why they are willing to die."

He looked puzzled. I bid him good day and drove away.

Who knows if he'll ever come to church or reconcile with people he thinks he hates, but that isn't my job. Mine is only to represent the Jesus of my salvation and plant seeds when and where I can. Perhaps there's another who will water them. Perhaps I will be called upon again.

The gospel message is a delicate matter these days. It seems that the color of my skin and admission of my faith is all it takes to generate hatred. Like many others, I try desperately not to get angry, but there is a place where righteous anger belongs. I displayed neither but did resolve to send a book to his address.

I find myself concerned about how the world views Christians these days. I fear I may not be able to say what I need to say because there is so much objection that I could only become the picture of what they think I am. "Christian" is no longer a respected term. It is hated and ridiculed in the world. I'm fairly clear on that. I expect it will get worse as evil imposes its will. I pray for opportunities and the courage to confront those who refuse to hear in a way that pleases God. It is difficult to distinguish the unchurched from the swine. I tend to hold my pearls until there is ample room to cast them.

I do know this: Young folks are at risk. I'd venture to say we have failed by not teaching them more about Jesus. It seems that there are so many obstacles to overcome. It takes so much to get to a place of actually explaining the message to them. Overcoming their now implanted teaching is a journey in and of itself, and our own are falling in line with them in an effort to reach out. I'm not going to be a party to that. I need to practice restraint where it's needed and courage where it is required. My prayers have become more personal.

I have become a Philistine in my own land. It's time I recognized this and became a better servant. Only God can save them. I'm just a soldier. The enemy is always out there, churning up trouble without mercy, and he literally charges when you least expect it.

Proverbs 29:22

A man of wrath stirs up strife, and one given to anger causes much transgression.

Screen Saver

I HAD THIS DREAM. You know, the one where you keep falling and falling. It was that one, only this time, I sorta soft landed on this path that appeared to be just this side of heaven. The place was beautiful like you'd expect, puffy clouds, birds singing, all of that. It was a typical dream sequence in a zip-a-dee-doo-dah kind of way. All I knew was that I was glad to be here.

I knew I was supposed to be here. I was kind of proud of myself, considering the odds. I knew it was all about Jesus, but still, there was great satisfaction knowing I had finally made it. I picked up the pace, walking at a half-jog like I owned the place, trying out the new body as it were.

There were people gathered on both sides of the pathway waving and welcoming me. I was wavin' back and yellin', "Hallelujah!" and shakin' hands and lookin' for anybody I might know. I recognized quite a few of them, but I kept going, headed for the gates in the distance.

I ran into a few former neighbors and friends. I'd visit with them later. I still had a ways to go, and right now, I was just happy to be here. I was movin' along at a pretty good pace. It was a long road, but I knew who was at the end of it, and that's who I needed to see.

Along the way, I caught glimpses of people I had known: old friends, co-workers, and neighbors, all laughin' and elbow nudgin' each other, pointin' at me and sayin' stuff like, "Ain't that a hoot. He made it!"

Just then, I saw a hand reachin' out from the crowd trying to shake my hand. It was my old preacher, pointin' and laughin' and yellin', "Welp! There goes the neighborhood!" I laughed and shook his hand. He'd been such a great gift to me.

A little further up, I saw my ex, shakin' her head, lookin' bewildered, and shoutin', "What are you doin' here?" She was smilin'. Hadn't seen that in a while. I responded by grabbing my chest in an overacting kinda way. "Will wonders never cease!" I smiled back and laughed. Anyway, I was glad to see she'd made it.

Lots of folks were there, even a few surprises; old Army buddies, teachers, classmates, and third cousins twice removed (removed from what I didn't know). It was a really nice reception. I knew I was gonna like heaven. This was great!

I just kept walkin', anxious to reach the end, lookin' forward to the eternity that awaited me, laughin' and yellin' back at all the people I recognized. Still, I wanted to meet Jesus. After all, He'd made all this possible.

As I moved along, I noticed that the noise and cheers were beginning to fade. The crowds had thinned, the voices had all but subsided, and I was suddenly aware that this may not be heaven at all. It was too quiet, still, lonely almost, disturbing and not at all like I'd imagined. Ahead I could see a sign that read simply: "Opportunities." I slowed my pace to a shuffle.

As I got closer, I saw large screens that had been erected on both sides of the path. They each flashed photos of people I had known in my lifetime, some briefly and some for many years. I stopped and stood there watching their faces, realizing that they were the faces of those I had never spoken to about Jesus or heaven or anything like that.

With every face, I started to realize that I could have said something or done something, been a little more loving, shined a little more light, or pointed to the one who saved me. Surely I could've done more than nothing!

As I watched the screen, stunned by the sheer number of faces, my initial feelings of jubilation turned to shame as each screen showed another face of someone I had known and someone I hadn't reached out to with a single message of hope. I shuddered as I thought of each one of them headed for an eternity separated from God.

The photos just kept comin'. I stared at the faces and wished I could have a second chance. I knew that was impossible. I realized my entire life had been more failures than successes. I started to see what a terrible example I'd been.

I began to weep as I moved past the familiar faces. I remembered those times when I was moved to talk to each one of them about what Jesus had done for me and for any who would believe. I became burdened with the thought of their eternity without Him.

I saw the gates ahead and began to wonder if they would remain open for me. I doubted I would gain entrance after seeing so many of my failures. I moved forward with the screens still flashing photos, too many to count. Regret overwhelmed me. I was ashamed, brokenhearted, and convicted, to say the least.

I walked through the open gates without any issues. The angel sentinels stared straight ahead. It almost felt like I'd snuck in.

Just ahead was a great hall with light emanating from within. The path gave way to golden streets. The air was clean and crisp. There were voices singing a new song. I knew at that moment that this was it, the place I had longed for. This was heaven! I was filled with an overwhelming sense of shame. I didn't know for sure that I'd be staying. How could I?

I entered the throne room and fell to my knees before the throne of the living God, feeling unworthy to even look into the face of Jesus. I begged His forgiveness for all the failures in my life and for all those people I ignored and all of those who would spend eternity in that place of suffering to which I must now be headed.

He interrupted my sobbing confession. With a soothing yet powerful voice, He said, "Oh, they're not all going to hell. Those photos are just the opportunities you missed. No one gets here without me, but you could've been a better example to them. That was what I called you to do. Instead, you never said anything to them."

"I know, Lord," I sputtered "I'm not worthy to be here. I failed you miserably. I understand now. I wish I could have stayed and done more. If I could just go back and tell them . . ."

"That won't be necessary. I've sent others to do the work. You're here because you believed in me and loved me. You read my book. You know what I promised. You know that I bought you for a price. So, come on in, my son. Nothing you ever did could have saved a single soul. I paid the price on that cross. The screens are nothing more than a reminder."

With that, I understood that all I had come to believe was true, that no one deserved heaven, especially me. Jesus paid it all. More importantly, I was saved by grace through faith, just as the Bible says.

I awoke from my dream, unsettled because I couldn't forget the faces flashing on that screen. I decided to use my second chance, even if the first was only a dream.

If you're reading this, it's because your face was one that flashed up on that screen. We may never have been introduced. We may have only briefly met. We may only be cyber friends, but I want for you what has been promised to each of us who surrender to Him. You're one who I don't want to forget and certainly, the Lord still has a plan and purpose for your life.

You should know this. There is a place called heaven. It's not a dream. It's a destination. Jesus is enthroned there, but He's here too. He's God, you see. He's everywhere at once. He loves you so much that He gave His life so that you could spend eternity with Him in a place He prepared for you.

John 5:24

Very truly I tell you, whoever hears my word and believes him who sent me has eternal life and will not be judged but has crossed over from death to life.

My prayer for you today:

I pray that someone will be so kind to you today that you will see the love of Jesus shining through them.

I pray that something so dramatic will occur in your life that you have absolutely no recourse but to sink to your knees and thank God for his grace and mercy.

I pray that God will show Himself to you in such a profound way that you will be forever changed and eternally grateful.

I pray that you will see God so clearly that you will seek Him more earnestly and love Him more passionately.

I pray that you will knock, and Jesus will burst into your life with an unrelenting presence.

I pray that your heart will be so filled with the love of God that you will aim higher, stand taller, and shine brighter.

I pray that you will find peace beyond understanding, love for all eternity, and hope beyond your own imagination.

I pray that you come into the presence of God and earnestly seek His will for your life.

I pray these things in the name above every other name, Jesus Christ!

Amen and amen.

It is my hope that you have enjoyed this book. I trust it has been helpful to you in some small way.

If you'd like to know more about our ministry, feel free to contact us via email with your questions or comments

Standrewjr@outlook.com

Other books available by Stan Drew, Jr.

CPSIA information can be obtained
at www.ICGtesting.com
Printed in the USA
BVHW082221041122
651160BV00002B/21